Applied Microeconomic Problems

Applied Microeconomic Problems

Rosemary Clarke

University of Birmingham

Philip Allan

First published 1985 by

PHILIP ALLAN PUBLISHERS LIMITED
MARKET PLACE
DEDDINGTON
OXFORD OX5 4SE

British Library Cataloguing in Publication Data

Clarke, Rosemary, 1933–
    Applied microeconomic problems.
    1. Microeconomics
    I. Title
    338.5   HB172

    ISBN 0-86003-056-3
    ISBN 0-86003-151-9 Pbk

Typeset by MHL Typesetting Ltd, Coventry
Printed and bound in Great Britain by The Camelot Press,
Southampton

Contents

Acknowledgements

During the past three years, when I have used many of these problems in teaching microeconomics, I have received much advice and help from many people, both students and colleagues in my own department and elsewhere in the University. I am particularly grateful to Paul Grout who has been very generous with both time and ideas, and to Roger Backhouse and Henry Scott who have helped to weed out mistakes and have made many useful suggestions. I would also like to thank the university library staff for their help and unfailing patience in dealing with numerous queries. I am indebted to them all: without their assistance, there would be many more errors and unclear passages.

My debt to the authors of various articles and books, who have provided ideas and source material for the problems, will be obvious. A special word of thanks is due to Amartya Sen for permission to reproduce Table 2 from his article, 'Starvation and exchange entitlements: a general approach and its application to the great Bengal famine', published by the Academic Press in the *Cambridge Journal of Economics* (1977), and to Chapman & Hall Limited for permission to make use of Table 1 and to reproduce Figures 1, 2 and 3 from the article, 'Risk preferences in Scandinavian shipping', by Peter Lorange and Victor Norman, published in *Applied Economics* (1973) .

The cover photographs have been reproduced by kind permission of Oxfam, Austin Rover and David Richardson.

Introduction

The major challenge in teaching microeconomics is to reconcile the theoretical models with the world we see around us. To many students the gap seems unbridgeable: microeconomics appears abstract and irrelevant to the problems of the 'real world'. Unless we can demonstrate that the theoretical models we teach can help us to understand this world, and guide us in choosing between potential courses of action, then it is not surprising that students lack motivation and fall back on memorising, rather than understanding, the theory.

For students the most difficult part of any economics course is making the leap between learning the theory and using it to analyse problems. Teachers have responded in different ways. The traditional method has been to refer students to articles for applications and to devise problems, often mathematical and abstract, to test their understanding of the theory. My experience is that while some students find this method helpful, many do not. The articles to which they are referred are usually written by professional economists for other economists and often the elementary microeconomic theory is not spelled out in sufficient detail for a second-year student to follow. Such articles leave a student wondering where the links are between the theory in textbooks and the problems analysed. One response to these difficulties has been the introduction of examples of applications into the textbooks. While this undoubtedly makes the books more readable for students and makes clearer the link between theory and problem, it does little to help them learn how to use the theory to analyse the problems they read about in the newspapers or encounter in their lives. Indeed one of the difficulties that any teacher of microeconomics faces is that while students easily recognise 'macroeconomic problems', microeconomic problems are harder to identify. Students do not readily appreciate that their micro-theory can help them to understand, for example, why fishing rights create difficulties in negotiating Spain's entry in the Common Market, or why OPEC has only recently started to introduce monitoring of quota arrangements within the cartel.

In this book I have put together a coherent set of problems which can be used throughout a second-year microeconomics course. Each chapter takes a problem and, by asking a series of leading questions, helps students to think this problem through, applying micro-theory as it goes along. The application of theory thus becomes an integral part of the course. Students have to think through each step in the analysis for themselves: they do not just see how theory is applied, but learn to use the theory as a tool. The book is neither a textbook nor a workbook. It is meant to be used alongside any of the currently available second-year microeconomic textbooks and has been designed for use in group discussion such as tutorials and classes. It is not a workbook as no answers are provided to the questions. This is deliberate: students learn the theory in lectures and by reading the textbooks. At some point, however, they must think through each new concept, each step in the analysis, for themselves, and not just follow someone else's exposition. By providing some leading questions, in an applied context, students have to think again about the theory they have studied. If answers were provided, human nature being what it is, at the first difficulty they would turn to them! Where an answer is not immediately to hand, the struggle to work out an answer becomes part of the learning process.

I would stress that the problems have been designed for use in tutorials or classes. At the start of each chapter I have provided a brief summary of the problem, together with a list of the key terms and theory to be used in the analysis. The choice of problems has been guided by the requirements of a second-year microeconomics course in order to ensure coverage of the theory. Some of the problems are based on published articles; others were suggested to me by some item in a newspaper. Discussion of applied topics often founders on students' unfamiliarity with the context of the problem. I have therefore provided sufficient background material, where necessary, to enable the student to complete the analysis without having to undertake further reading. Each problem is self-contained but I have tried to link it with published work on the topic, and references for supplementary reading are given at the end of each chapter. These do not need to be followed up unless the student is interested in reading further.

It is desirable that students prepare for the group discussion by reading through the problem beforehand in order to familiarise themselves with any background material and also to gain an over-view of the topic. Some of the questions are straightforward, requiring application of theory covered in lectures and textbooks. Other questions are more difficult and, as the analysis progresses, raise wider issues to which there is often no one 'right' answer. Group discussion can help students develop a better understanding of theory and its use and, at the same time, provide a forum for discussion of the more general questions.

In some problems diagrams have been left blank. This has been done to encourage students to construct and complete diagrams for themselves. It is only when they do this that they begin to understand the diagrams. In some cases, one diagram has to be derived from another and when this is necessary, the diagrams have been aligned (for example one below another) so that the links can be recognised. At other times, as the analysis proceeds, diagrams are built up step by step, and here again blank diagrams have been left in the appropriate pages so that a record can be kept of the stages in the analysis.

Finally, I would address a few words directly to any student who has read this far in the Introduction. The aim throughout this book is to get you to use micro-theory and to think for yourself. Working through these problems and thinking out the answers can be hard work and there will be times when you will find yourself stuck for an answer: this is when the classes will help. You will get more out of the class if you have read through the problem beforehand and thought about the questions. In order to help you to make a start on your own, I have listed the key concepts that you will need in the analysis at the beginning of each problem. This gives you a hint on what to prepare and what to revise if your understanding of the theory is shaky. If, after the class, you are still not sure that you have understood all the points raised, then you should go back to your lecture notes or your textbook to check your understanding of the relevant theory. If your difficulty does not arise from a failure to understand the theory, then it may help you to follow up on the supplementary reading which is suggested at the end of the chapter. Some students also find it useful to set up a study group with fellow students. Working through this set of problems is a more demanding way to study microeconomics than limiting your reading to a textbook but, if you persevere, the rewards will be a better understanding of the theory, greater confidence in your ability to think for yourself, and, most satisfying of all, the feeling that you have achieved something by yourself and have not just absorbed information like blotting paper. If you are prepared to put in the effort, I am sure that you will agree that microeconomics does have a lot to say about the world we live in.

1

Rationing to Restrict Demand

In this problem we consider when a government might resort to rationing a good and examine whether people should be allowed to trade their ration coupons. In order to analyse these questions you will need to understand how equilibrium of demand and supply is achieved. Before starting to work through the problem, be sure you also understand the following:

(a) *the conditions for the optimum of the consumer;*
(b) *how to derive these conditions using the Lagrange multiplier;*
(c) *how to find a consumer's demand function from the utility function;*
(d) *the difference between slack and binding constraints.*

Question 1 If a good is suddenly in short supply, should the market be left to allocate the good through the price mechanism or should the government intervene? If you think the government should intervene, then you have to consider what form intervention should take. Before doing this, however, make a note of what happens to price and profits if no intervention occurs. Draw a diagram illustrating your conclusions.

Question 2 What forms of intervention could the government adopt?

Question 3 What criteria would you suggest to provide guidance on when intervention is appropriate? For example, would you argue that a severe shortage of, say, whisky or potatoes should be handled in the same manner? And what about a shortage of oil?

Question 4 During the oil crisis of 1973/74, petrol coupons were distributed to all car owners in this country but, as it turned out, they were not used and no *formal* rationing

1

scheme was put into operation. Can you think how rationing may occur informally?

Question 5 When the ration coupons were issued, there was discussion whether or not to allow trading of the coupons. The majority view in the House of Commons was that trading should be illegal. In the United States the general view was that if formal rationing were introduced (it wasn't), trading should be permitted. What is your view?

Question 6 The main argument put forward in the UK to support prohibition of coupon trading was that it would be unfair to low-income consumers. What do you think of this argument?

This argument can be evaluated using the basic model of consumer behaviour where a consumer maximises utility subject to one or more constraints.

Question 7 Suppose that there are two consumers who are alike in all respects except that one has a larger income than the other. As they have identical tastes and preferences, they both have the same utility function,

$$u(X, Y) = XY$$

where X and Y represent the amounts of two goods consumed in a given time period. The price of X is £6 a unit and that of Y is £4 a unit. (Prices are chosen to keep calculations simple rather than to indicate a pessimistic view of future petrol prices!) R is richer than P and has a budget of £120 as against P's budget of £60. Find the two consumers' utility maximising consumption levels before rationing is introduced.

Question 8 Now suppose that X is suddenly in short supply and it is decided that formal rationing should be introduced. Each consumer is issued with a total of 12 ration points and the ration point 'price' of X is set by the government at two points. Trading of ration coupons is forbidden and both R and P are law-abiding citizens who would not operate in a black market. (Do you think that a black market might develop? If you do, explain why.) Find R's and P's optimum consumption levels now that X is rationed.

(*Hint*: Remember that R and P are now maximising utility subject to *two* constraints. Before you work out their optimum bundles, think very carefully whether R and P will spend all their budget and all their ration points. Put another way, will both constraints always be binding at the consumer's optimum? Sketch a few diagrams to illustrate possible outcomes. After doing this I think you will see that while it is possible that the solution might be where both constraints are binding, there is also the possibility that only one of the two constraints will be binding.)

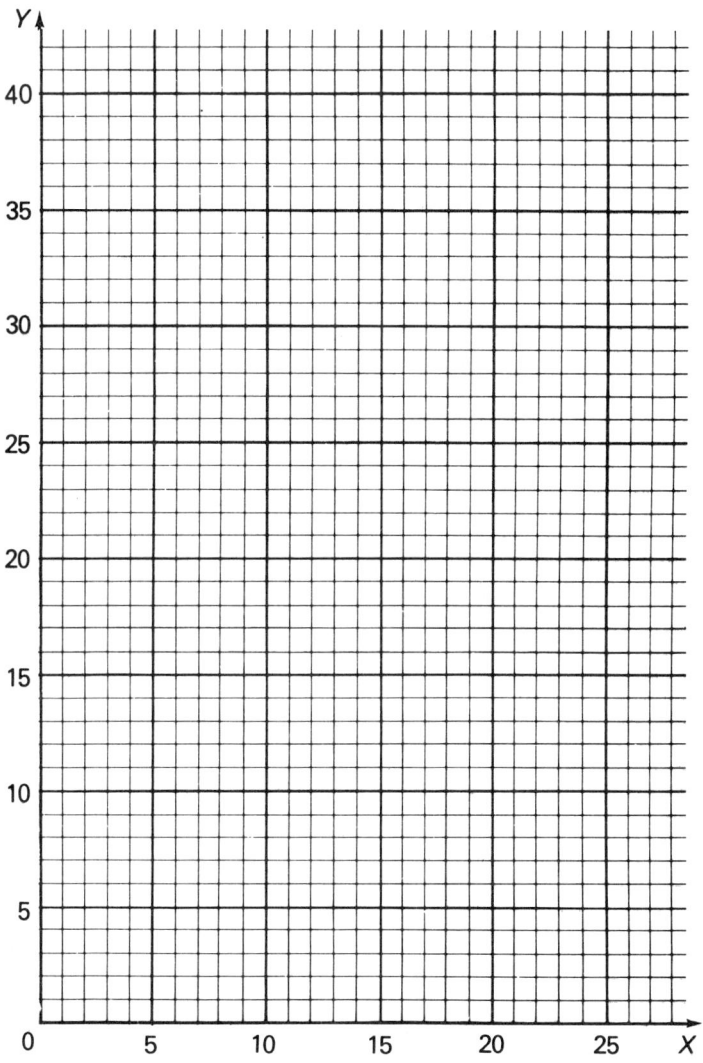

Figure 1.1

Question 9 On Figure 1.1, draw in the budget and ration constraints for R and P. (There is plenty of room for both
on the same diagram but you might like to use different
colours for the two consumers to make it clearer.) Mark
clearly the area which contains all bundles available to
each consumer given his constraints, and show the quantities of X and Y consumed before and after the
introduction of rationing.

Question 10 Following the introduction of rationing, will each consumer's utility increase if he is given one more ration
point or one more pound? What do the equilibrium
values of the Lagrangian multipliers represent?

Question 11 (a) Assume now that trading of ration coupons is permitted and that a perfect market exists with the market
clearing price for ration coupons being £1. (What determines the price of ration coupons?) Find both consumers' optimum consumption bundles. Draw the new
'combined' constraint for each consumer on Figure 1.1
and show the new optima.
(*Hint*: When a market exists, one coupon point can be
exchanged for £1.00. This means that consumers can now
(legally) convert points into pounds or vice versa and thus a
consumer will now optimise subject to one constraint. In order
to derive this constraint we need to convert the price of X (and
the consumer's income) into 'total effective pounds' or 'total
effective points'. The effective pound price of X is equal to the
pound price plus number of coupons required multiplied by
£1.00. (What is the effective point price of X and Y
respectively?) Work out the relevant effective prices (in pounds
or points) and do not forget to work out R's and P's effective
incomes.)
(b) You should find that the two consumers' utility
levels are greater under a rationing system which permits trading in coupons than under one when trading is
forbidden. Explain in your own words why *both* consumers are better off with trading.

Question 12 Would it be correct to say that rationing with legal
trading of coupons means that all units of the rationed
good have the same opportunity cost?

Question 13 Does coupon trading encourage or discourage a consumer to economise on the scarce good?

Question 14 With legal trading of coupons, the allocation of twelve
coupons was effectively a gift of additional income from
the government. What was the value of this income
supplement?

Postcript: I wonder if it occurred to you that you could save time by
estimating R's and P's demand functions from your answer to Question 7.
Then, instead of having to work through the whole Lagrangian method to
get answers to Questions 8 and 11, you could substitute the new 'prices' and
'incomes' into each consumer's demand function to get the optimum consumption levels of X and Y. If this did not occur to you, before you move on
from this exercise make sure that you know how to derive the demand functions for X and Y.

2

Some Further Points on Rationing

This exercise builds on your work in Problem 1. We shall extend our analysis of how the government might intervene in the market when a good is suddenly in short supply by comparing two possible options: rationing and the introduction of an excise tax. The obvious difference between these two options is that, whereas rationing is likely to be accompanied by price controls on the good in question, an excise tax 'rations' through the price mechanism. Clearly, the two methods have different implications for income distribution and we examine how the government might offset any regressive impact of an excise tax by coupling it with an income rebate.

Before you start on this problem, make sure you understand the following:

(a) *the consumer's budget constraint;*
(b) *how income and price expansion paths are derived;*
(c) *income elasticity of demand;*
(d) *price elasticity of demand;*
(e) *the income and substitution effects of a price change.*

Question 1 Can you think why an excise tax might be preferred to a market solution when a good is suddenly in short supply? Would the long-run supply implications be the same in each case?

Question 2 Before going any further, list what you consider are the main arguments for and against an excise tax when compared with rationing. Make clear the type of rationing scheme you are considering (e.g. will coupons be tradeable?) and which scheme you consider would be the most costly to administer.

At this point, before comparing alternative schemes, we will first check that we can show the excise tax, and the tax revenue generated, on a diagram. Figure 2.1 shows the budget constraint of a representative consumer and her optimum consumption bundle (point A). The axes are labelled X, representing petrol, and Y, representing expenditure on all other goods. Assuming that the consumer does not save, then OM is equal to income. (Alternatively, we can assume that OM represents the consumer's budget allocation for consumption goods.)

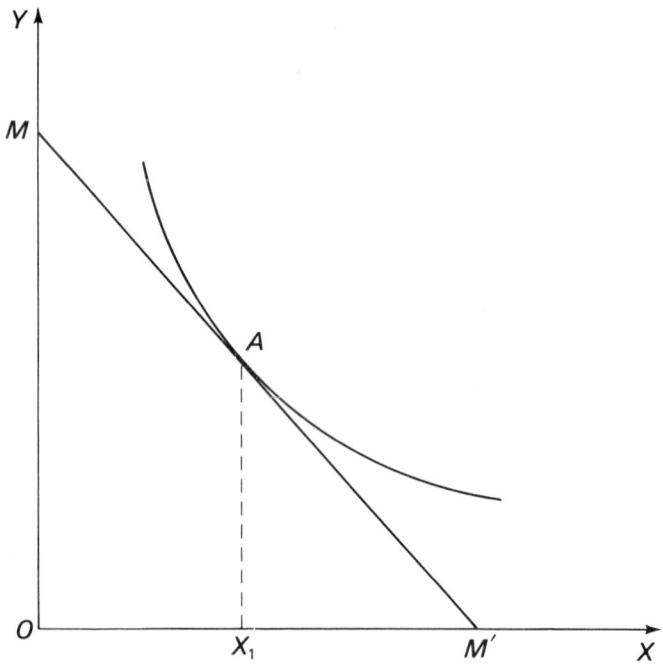

Figure 2.1

Question 3 Before you start on the next few questions, think whether you consider petrol to be a normal good. What information would you need in order to ascertain this?

Question 4 In Figure 2.1, the consumer is shown to be purchasing X_1 units of petrol. How much of her income has she had to give up to purchase these units? How much income is left for the purchase of other goods?

Question 5 Suppose that the government now introduces an excise tax, amounting to 25 per cent of the current price. (To keep things simple we shall assume that prior to the shortage, petrol was untaxed.) Draw in the appropriate schedule on Figure 2.1. Draw a new consumer optimum and show on the diagram the amount of tax revenue that would be raised.

Question 6 Now show that different levels of excise tax will yield different amounts of tax revenue. Why is this the case?

Question 7 If you draw a curve joining up the various consumer optima shown on your diagram, what have you plotted?

We now push a little deeper into our analysis of an excise tax as a rationing device. Rationing by points, when there is a shortage of a good that is widely consumed and considered a necessity, is often thought to be fairer than price rationing, as people on low incomes can be assured a share in the restricted supply. Consideration of the income effects which arise from the use of an excise tax might lead the government to consider returning the revenue raised by this tax to consumers, thus mitigating some of these income effects. What would be the implications of adopting such refunds? The next two questions examine this possibility.

Question 8 (a) Suppose that in Period 1 the government introduces an excise tax which reduces consumption of petrol to X_s. This is shown in Figure 2.2. Label the amount of tax revenue generated once you have drawn in the appropriate schedule.
(b) At the end of the period all this tax revenue is returned to the consumer as an income supplement. (We assume there are no administrative costs.) Will the consumer be as well off as before?
(c) In Period 2 the tax remains at the same level as in Period 1 and, at the end of Period 2, the tax revenue is once again refunded to the consumer. Will the consumer's optimum bundle after the refund be the same bundle as in (b)?
(d) If the excise tax remains the same and the government continues to return the tax revenue to the consumer, when will the consumer's optimum bundle also be her equilibrium bundle?

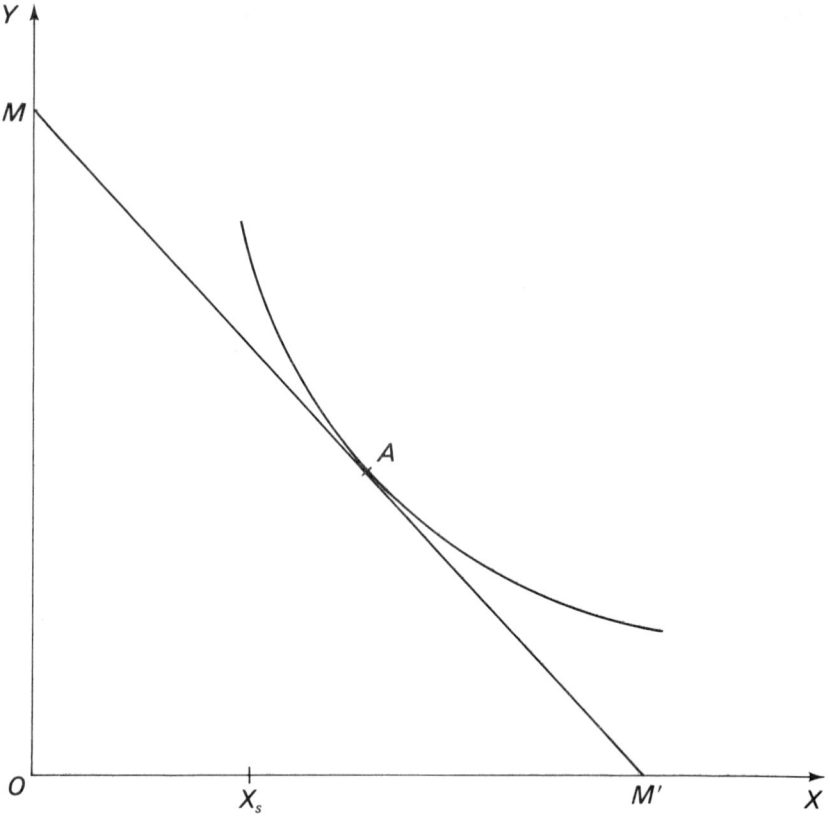

Figure 2.2

(e) Even though all the tax revenue paid by the consumer is returned to her, she is now less well off than
before. Explain why.

From your answers to Question 8 you can see that if the government uses
an excise tax as a rationing device, but returns the tax revenue to consumers,
consumption of the scarce good is reduced by a smaller amount than would
be the case if the revenue were not returned to the consumer.

Question 9 Consider now whether it is possible for the government
to restrict consumption so that it *does not exceed quantity* X_s and, at the same time, keep consumers at their
original utility level by means of an income supplement.

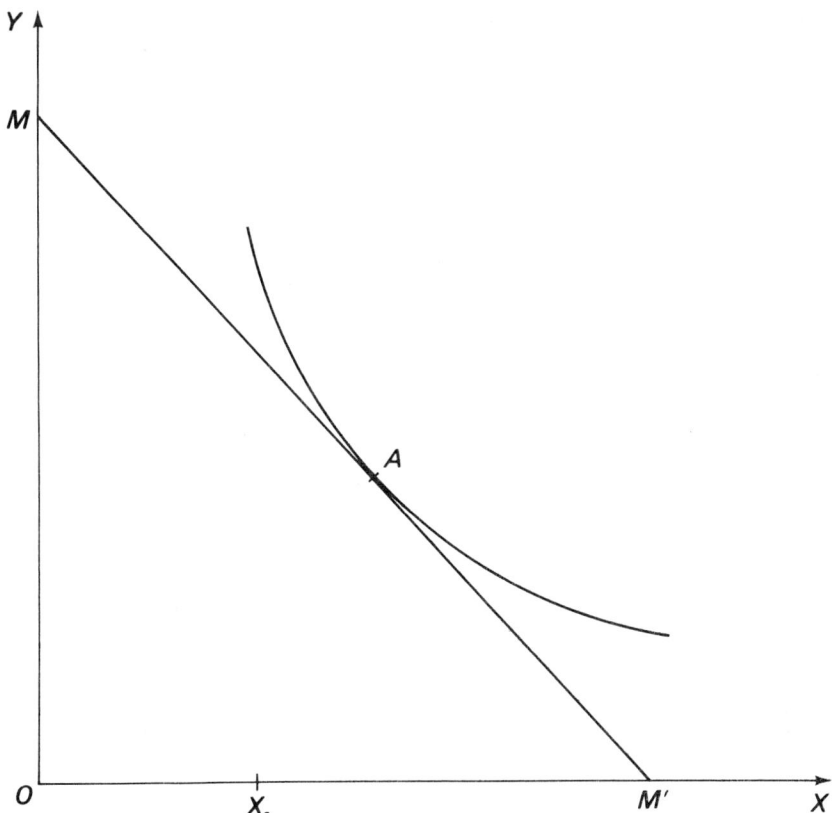

Figure 2.3

(a) Use Figure 2.3 to illustrate how the government could do this.

(b) Is the tax revenue generated by the excise tax sufficient to cover the cost of the income supplement?

(c) Mark the income expansion path on your diagram. Does it show X as a normal good?

Question 10 Having explored the combined tax/income supplement option, we now compare it with a rationing scheme where coupon trading is permitted. Our examination of these two options will make use of the work you did for the previous problem, 'Rationing to Restrict Demand'. In Figure 2.4 we have drawn the budget and ration constraints of individual R, in accordance with the information provided in Questions 7 and 8 of Problem 1.

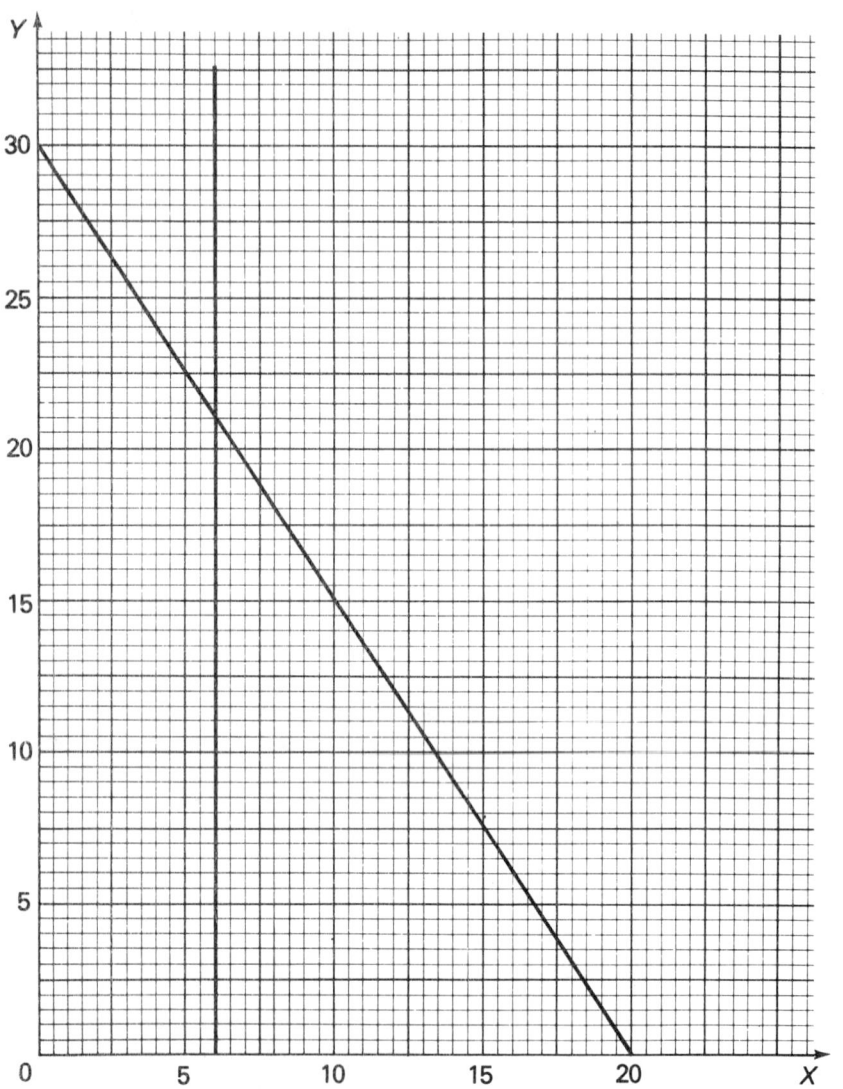

Figure 2.4

(a) When coupons are transferable we know that these two constraints become one. Using your answer to Question 11 in the previous exercise, draw in this constraint and show R's optimum bundle when coupon trading is permitted.

(b) Suppose that instead of introducing rationing, the government levied an excise tax on good X which raised its price to £8 a unit, i.e. to a price equal to X's effective price when rationed. Draw in the appropriate constraint and show the consumer's optimum bundle (remember — there is now no rationing by coupons).

(c) In addition to introducing the excise tax, the government gives each consumer an income supplement of £12.00. What is the consumer's optimum bundle now?

(d) Repeat this exercise for individual P and find whether the tax revenue received from P and R is sufficient to cover the income supplements.

(e) If it is intended to achieve the same level of consumption of the scarce good under both schemes, why must the amount of income redistributed from the tax revenue be related to the coupon allocation and not to the amount of petrol consumed prior to the introduction of the excise tax?

(f) In answering these questions (and questions in the previous exercise) we took the market price of coupons as £1.00 per coupon. Now work out from your answer to (a) above, how many coupons R and P would have bought or sold at this price. If R and P were the only consumers trading coupons, would this price be an equilibrium price?

Question 11 Walter Salant, comparing rationing with the tax/income supplement scheme, concludes that:

(t)he only inherent difference between the two systems, apart from costs of administration, is that rationing with transferable coupons fixes the total quantity that may be bought and allows the price increase (in the form of the price of coupons) corresponding to that quantity to be determined in the market, while the excise tax method allows the quantity to be settled in the market. (Salant 1979, p. 160)

Would you agree with him?

Salant's article is a theoretical analysis of the two schemes. Carol Dahl uses American data for 1978 to compare a rationing scheme with an excise tax, but no income supplement.[1]

1. Archibald and Gillingham (1981) also compare the distributional effects of the two schemes.

At that time petrol sold for $0.655 a gallon and the quantity demanded was 114.21 billion gallons a year (Dahl 1984, p. 25). If an oil crisis had developed, it was believed that demand would have had to be reduced to 107.31 billion gallons. Under rationing, and assuming the market price fixed at $0.655 a gallon of petrol, Dahl estimates the 'effective' market clearing price would have been $0.920, implying a coupon price of $0.265. If an excise tax had been adopted instead of rationing, the market clearing price would have been $0.892 (op. cit., p. 29).[2]

Question 12 Why is the market clearing price lower for an excise tax than a rationing scheme?
(*Hint*: remember she considers the case of an excise tax without an income supplement.)

Carol Dahl concludes that the rationing scheme would have been progressive (that is to say that the income changes were less harsh on the lower income groups), whereas the tax scheme would have been regressive. However, the rationing scheme would have been much more costly.

References

Archibald, R. and Gillingham, R. (1981) 'The distributional impact of alternative gasoline conservation policies', *Bell Journal of Economics*, 12, pp. 426—444.
* Dahl, Carol A. (1984) 'Vertical equity effects and total consumer losses for emergency allocation schemes for the gasoline market', *Applied Economics*, 16, pp. 25—32.
* Salant, Walter S. (1979) 'Rationing and price as methods of restricting demand for specific products', in M.J. Boskin (ed.), *Economics and Human Welfare: Essays in Honor of Tibor Scitovsky*, Academic Press.

---

2. Taking a higher estimate of income elasticity, the 'effective' market clearing price of petrol would be $0.761, implying a coupon price of $0.106; with taxation the relevant market price would be $0.741 (op. cit., p. 31).

* Suggested supplementary reading.

3

Life in 2029: Part I

In this two-part problem we extend our model of consumer behaviour to consider how an individual allocates resources over his or her lifetime. In Part I we start by asking why people save and then examine the life-cycle model of consumption (and savings) behaviour. We finish by considering how an imperfect capital market may affect an individual's consumption function.

Before you start on the problem, make sure you understand the following:

(a) *what is meant by the endowment position of the consumer;*
(b) *the distinction between income and wealth;*
(c) *the inter-temporal optimum of the consumer;*
(d) *the rate of time preference;*
(e) *the consumption function.*

People save for various reasons (can you think of some?) but probably the major reasons are (i) precautionary and (ii) to maintain their standard of living following retirement. Income and consumption flows will not necessarily coincide at different periods of one's life: generally one would expect an individual's income to be fairly low early in life, to rise over his working life (possibly levelling out in later years) and to fall on retirement. However, unexpected events may also result in a fall in earned income at any time during one's working life (can you think of examples of such events?).

Question 1 What do you think *your* lifetime earnings profile looks like in the light of your current expectations? Plot it roughly on Figure 3.1. If you want to maintain a constant (or rising) standard of living, how could you achieve this?

15

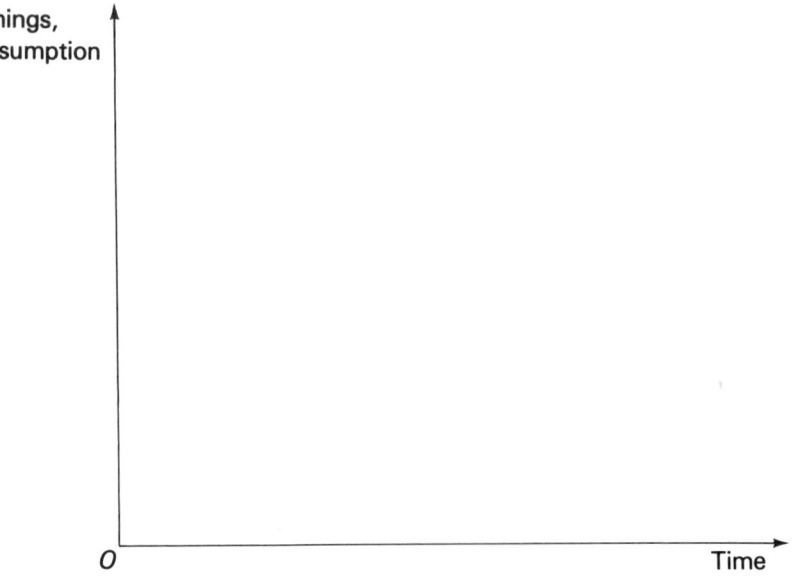

Figure 3.1

Figure 3.2

Question 2 The life-cycle model of consumption behaviour assumes that an individual is forward looking and plans his optimal consumption over his lifetime, given his lifetime budget constraint (Modigliani and Brumberg 1954; Ando and Modigliani 1963; Hicks 1939). In general, we assume that the individual leaves no debts on his death (though he can leave bequests) so that the budget constraint means that the present value of lifetime consumption does not exceed the present value of lifetime income and inherited wealth. Write down the utility function and the budget constraint of the individual implied by this model.

Question 3 Lifetime income can come from earnings and/or savings. The budget constraint states that expenditure must not exceed the present value of earned income plus the present value of any assets which the individual owns or acquires during his lifetime. Many assets yield an income stream but others may yield a consumption flow, rather than an income flow, while appreciating in capital value. Can you think of examples of such assets? In what form do you think most people hold their wealth?

Question 4 What are the major assumptions that underlie the life-cycle model of consumer behaviour? (List the main assumptions now; we will return to them later.)

Question 5 In order to simplify the model, assume that a consumer is concerned with only two periods: in Period 1 he earns Y_1 and in Period 2 he earns Y_2, where $Y_2 < Y_1$. Write down his utility function and budget constraint. Using the Lagrange multiplier method, derive the conditions for his optimum consumption levels in the two periods, assuming that he faces a perfect capital market, i.e. he can borrow or lend at the same real rate of interest, r.

Question 6 List the variables which determine his consumption level in Period 1.

Question 7 Now suppose that there are two individuals, A and B, who each have the earnings profile set out in Question 5. Individual A saves at the current rate of interest but B has a positive (or more positive) time preference rate when compared with A and is a borrower. On Figure 3.2 show both A's and B's indifference maps (or a few

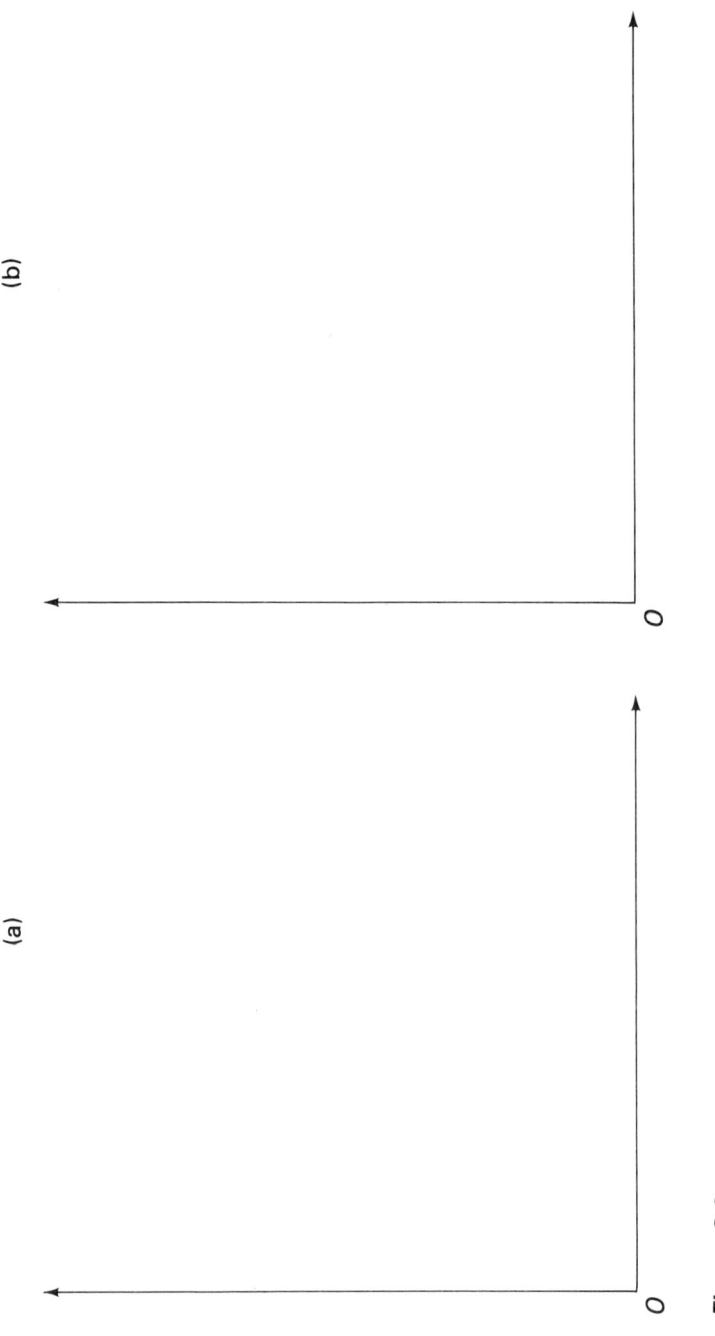

Figure 3.3

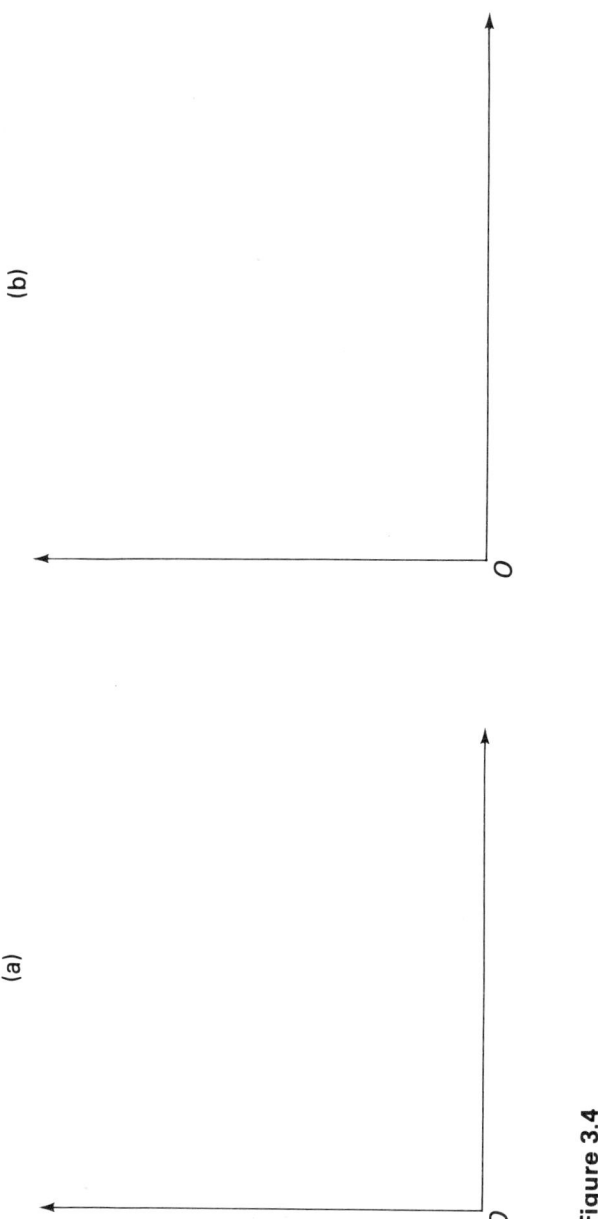

Figure 3.4

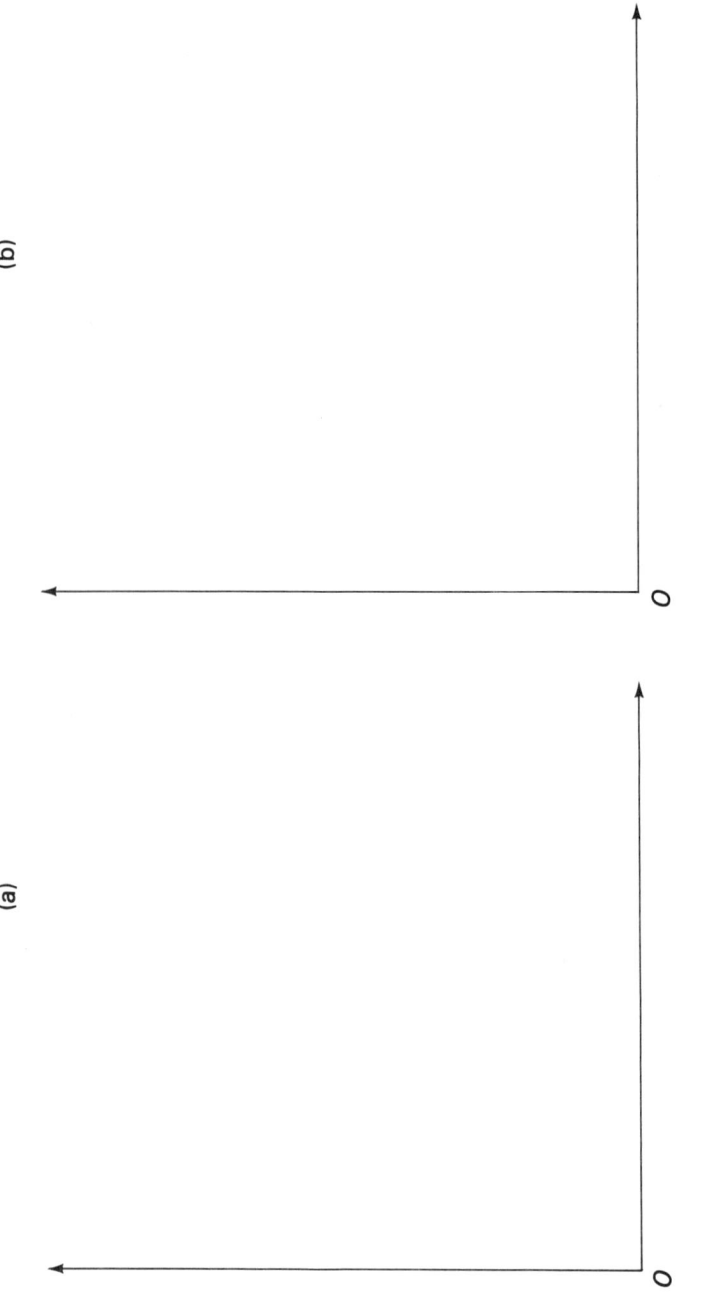

Figure 3.5

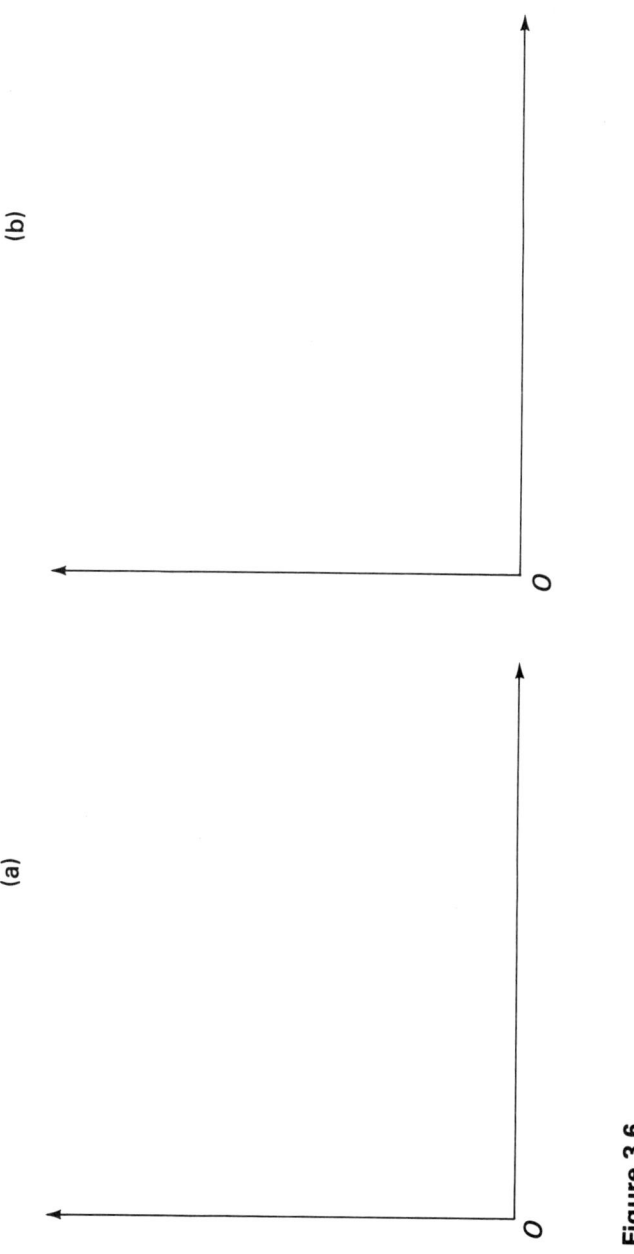

Figure 3.6

indifference curves for each of them) and label the indifference curves appropriately, as well as the axes. What
is meant by 'time preference rate'?

Question 8 Now draw two diagrams (use Figure 3.3), one for A and
one for B, showing their optimal consumption levels on
the assumption they face a perfect capital market. Show
clearly the amount of saving or dissaving. Be sure to
label the axes.

Question 9 Holding Y_2 constant, increase the income received in
Period 1 and trace out the consumption expansion paths
of A and B on Figure 3.3, (a) and (b). Using the
information in Figure 3.3, now plot the appropriate
consumption functions for A and B on Figure 3.4, (a)
and (b).

Question 10 We now drop the assumption that there is a perfect
capital market. In general we observe that the rate of
interest is higher for borrowers than it is for savers.
Why might this be? What will the budget constraints for
A and B look like when this is the case? Draw these on
Figure 3.3, (a) and (b). Will the individuals' optimum
consumption levels change?

Question 11 Will the consumption functions for A and B be the same
as when they faced a perfect capital market? Show any
change on Figure 3.4, (a) and (b).

Question 12 What difference would it make if it were impossible to
borrow? Draw appropriate diagrams for A and B,
showing their consumption expansion paths and consumption functions on Figures 3.5 and 3.6.

Providing there is no borrowing constraint, individuals may be borrowers, savers, or neither, at different times in their lives. The life-cycle
model of consumer behaviour suggests that a typical consumer will borrow
to finance consumption in his early working years and then save to maintain
consumption levels when earned income falls on retirement. If the consumer
had perfect knowledge, he could work out what amount he would need to
save in order to finance consumption during retirement but, of course, he
faces uncertainty about how long he will live, how long he will work (he may
fall sick or become unemployed), how secure an investment his asset purchases will turn out to be and how the rate of inflation will change over his
lifetime. In the model above, we implicitly assumed that a consumer knew
when he would die, how long he could work, etc. Did you spot this in your
answer to Question 4?

Question 13 Would you expect uncertainty about the following to
increase or decrease savings?

    (a) Date of death
    (b) Length of working life
    (c) Future rates of inflation

The life-cycle model thus assumes that individuals can make what amounts to a very difficult decision in planning optimum consumption patterns over their lifetimes. Moreover, as we have seen, if some people face capital market constraints, they may not be able to borrow. One study, using Canadian data to test the life-cycle model, found that the majority of people in the sample did accumulate savings over their lifetime but a significant group did not, and not all of the people in this group were young, i.e. people who might have been expected to have few assets (King and Dicks-Mireaux 1982; see also Diamond 1977). Some people, it seems, do not save or save only small amounts. Our current state of knowledge cannot explain all aspects of savings behaviour: it may be that some people find the problem too difficult for them to resolve; they may make mistakes; or they may have very high positive time preference rates. For some people social security is their only form of saving. By paying national insurance contributions during their working life, they are eligible for the retirement pension (and other benefits, e.g. unemployment, sickness). Of course, if social security did not exist, many of these people would have saved something. Nevertheless, more than half of the poor in this country are elderly people, and half of these have little or no income apart from their retirement pensions from the state scheme (Royal Commission on the Distribution of Income and Wealth 1978, Ch. 10).

In the second part of this problem we shall examine possible explanations as to why the state provides social security. Having done this, we shall then consider the effect of social security schemes on the amount of saving.

References

Ando, A. and Modigliani, F. (1963) 'The 'life cycle' hypothesis of saving: aggregate implications and tests', *American Economic Review*, 53, pp. 55–85.

Diamond, P.A. (1977) 'A framework for social security analysis', *Journal of Public Economics*, 8, pp. 275–298.

*Flemming, J.S. (1973) 'The consumption function when capital markets are imperfect: the permanent income hypothesis reconsidered', *Oxford Economic Papers*, 25, pp. 160–172.

Hicks, J.R. (1939) *Value and Capital*, Oxford University Press.

King, M.A. and Dicks-Mireaux, L. (1982) 'Asset holdings and the life cycle', *Economic Journal*, 92, pp. 247–267.

Modigliani, F. and Brumberg, R.E. (1954) 'Utility analysis and the consumption function', in K.K. Kirihara (ed.), *Post-Keynesian Economics*, Rutgers University Press.

Royal Commission on the Distribution of Income and Wealth (1978), Layard, R. *et al.*, Background Paper No. 5, *The Causes of Poverty*, HMSO.

---

* Suggested supplementary reading.

4

Life in 2029: Part II

We continue our analysis of the allocation of resources over time by making use of the simple two-period model we studied in Part I. The question we ask is: does the introduction of state social security result in an increase or a decrease in the amount of personal savings available for investment purposes? The basic theory required for this analysis has already been covered in Part I. We do, however, introduce some concepts that may be new to you. First of all, there is the notion of market failure. *By this we mean the possibility that the market may fail to provide those goods and services which consumers want and are prepared to pay for. Such failure may be absolute in that a market may not exist for some goods and services, or it may be that a market exists but the price at which producers are prepared to offer the good or service for sale does not reflect the opportunity cost of producing it, i.e. its marginal cost. There are various reasons why markets may fail: in this problem we learn that one cause may be the lack of perfect information. When information is unequally distributed between buyers and sellers, as in the insurance market, there are problems of* adverse selection *and* moral hazard. *If you have not come across these terms before, don't worry — they are explained in pages 28 and 29. It may take a little while to assimilate these new ideas, so it would be a good idea to read through the first few pages of the problem several times before you try to answer Questions 1 to 6. After you have done this, the rest of the problem should be plain sailing; if it is not, then think again about the model studied in Problem 3 and about the conditions for the inter-temporal optimum of the consumer.*

At the end of the first part of this exercise we noted that for some people in Britain their only income in retirement comes from the state retirement pension. If we ask why the state provides social security, one possible explanation is paternalism. The government compels people to save by contributing to social security so that they will have something to live on in their old age and people who are myopic, i.e. have very high positive time preference rates, are forced to save 'for their own good'.

Another explanation that we should consider is whether the market provides the savings options that individuals want. If it does not, should the state step in to fill the gap?

You will remember we noted that individuals are uncertain about the length of their retirement and about future inflation rates. What would be the ideal asset to purchase in order to be sure of a comfortable old age, given these uncertainties? Obviously a highly desirable asset would be an indexed annuity. Social security is, in effect, an annuity which most governments link in some degree to the cost of living. The UK government also issues index-linked bonds which are now generally available, although originally they could only be purchased by people over sixty.

Question 1   (a) What is an annuity? Is there a market in indexed annuities?
(b) Do occupational pension schemes provide a satisfactory form of saving for retirement for men and women?

The other kind of uncertainty a consumer faces is the risk that one's working life might be shortened because of illness or unemployment. While one can insure one's life, it is not currently possible to purchase unemployment insurance in the market. In the past, however, trade unions provided a form of unemployment insurance and this coverage was often an important reason for joining a union. Can we be sure that the market will always provide the insurance cover that people want? The answer is that it may not, the reason being that information is imperfect.

Consider a man who is contemplating taking out life insurance. Life insurance provides some financial security for his family in the event of his death and, until the 1984 Budget, provided an attractive form of saving as up to that time contributions were eligible for tax relief. If he takes out insurance on his life, he enters into a contract with an insurance company in which he contracts to make regular payments over a specified period of time while the company promises to pay an agreed sum either at the end of the period or, in the event of his death, during the period.

There are various transaction costs associated with the provision of such contracts: the insurance company faces administrative costs in preparing and drawing up the contract, monitoring costs in ascertaining that claims are genuine, etc. These transaction costs arise in part because of the uncertainty about the degree of risk associated with each purchaser of insurance. In our example, there are difficulties in estimating the probability of the insured surviving the term of the insurance. The insurance company has to make an estimate of this probability in order to decide whether to offer the insurance and at what premium.

Question 2 What factors do you think the insurance company will consider?
(a) List some factors which affect an individual's life expectancy.
(b) Which of these factors are outside of the individual's control?
(c) Which can be controlled to a greater or lesser extent by the individual?
(d) How easily can the insurance company obtain accurate information on the factors you have listed?
(e) Should a non-smoker expect to pay a lower premium for life insurance, other things being equal?

The essence of the insurance problem is that information about the factors which affect the probability of the event occurring is unequally distributed between the parties. Neither party knows for certain when the person requiring insurance is going to die (an exception is a suicide and most insurance policies specifically exclude cover on death from suicide); however, the insured generally has the more accurate estimate and certainly has a better knowledge of his life style. The insurers can determine fairly easily some of the characteristics which affect an individual's life expectancy but there will be others they cannot know without a good deal of costly investigation. Insurers may therefore decide that they can only offer life insurance at a uniform premium for individuals grouped in easily identified categories such as age and sex. These uniform premiums will be averaged premiums calculated on the basis of the insurers' experience for insured individuals in the different categories.

The other problem facing an insurer is that while some characteristics are outside the control of the insured, others are not, and an insured person may modify his behaviour once insurance coverage has been obtained. For example, age is not something an individual can control but lifestyle is. Smoking, diet, exercise — all these affect life expectancy but an individual's incentive to live a healthy life style may weaken once he has obtained cover to protect his family.

These two features, the unequal distribution of information and the possibility that the insured can change his behaviour in response to insurance coverage, give rise to two problems common to insurance contracts for diverse forms of cover. These problems are (i) adverse selection and (ii) moral hazard.

Adverse Selection

Consider a situation where all characteristics affecting the probability of an event are *outside* the insured's control. If some of these characteristics are difficult to determine, either the insurers will decide that the transaction costs are too high to justify providing cover, or they will offer the insurance if the costs are not so high as to outweigh any gains from the transaction. However, given the high costs of discovering details of some characteristics for each potential customer, the insurers offer cover at an averaged premium. People who are low risks (i.e. have low probability of the event occurring) will be faced with a higher-than-fair premium while the high-risk people obtain a lower-than-fair premium. Now people considering taking out insurance are generally better informed than the insurance company as to whether they constitute a high or low risk. The averaged premium may not attract low-risk individuals (even if they are risk averse) as they might consider it too high. High-risk people, however, are likely to take out the insurance at such a premium. In due course the insurers will find that their claim experience is greater than they had anticipated and they will find it necessary to raise the premium and the process is repeated. Now, in general, one would not expect people to fall into two categories of risk: high and low. When risks are distributed over a range of loss probabilities, the problem of adverse selection is reduced: the claims experience of the insurers will be improved and the average premium will attract more low-risk persons.

Question 3 Suppose that a company decides to enter an insurance market and provides identical cover to existing companies but charges a lower averaged premium. What claims experience might it meet?

Question 4 Will a state social security pension scheme suffer from the problem of adverse selection?

Moral Hazard

We also mentioned that an individual may be able to change the probability of the event occurring. In this case, insurance cover may actually provide an incentive for the insured to modify factors affecting the probability of the event as it may be to his advantage to do this.

Question 5 (a) What would be the effect of moral hazard on premiums?
(b) Does unemployment insurance raise the problems of adverse selection and moral hazard?
(c) What transaction costs would insurers face in offering unemployment insurance?
(d) Are the problems the same for private and state unemployment insurance?

Question 6 Do you think that government provision of social security can be explained and justified in terms of market failure?

If it were not for social security, it is clear that many low earners would have little to live on in retirement. For some people social security is a form of compulsory savings. For other people who save voluntarily, the question arises whether social security savings are a substitute for personal savings and whether, with the availability of social security, such people save more or less than they would otherwise have done. This is the problem analysed by Martin Feldstein (1974) in his article entitled, 'Social security, induced retirement, and aggregate capital accumulation'. Using a two period model, similar to the one we examined in Part I of this problem, Feldstein examines the impact of social security on an individual's lifetime savings.

Most men retire from work at the age of 65. In Figure 4.1, adapted from Feldstein's article, we measure income, consumption and saving up to the age of 65 on the horizontal axis. Income, etc., after 65 is measured on the vertical axis. To keep the analysis simple, Feldstein assumes that:

(i) pre-tax income before age 65 is not affected by the introduction of social security;

(ii) the rate of interest on social security savings is the same as that an individual could obtain on other forms of savings.

Question 7 We start by assuming that the individual retires at age
65 and has no earned income in his retirement period so
that consumption must be financed from savings made
during his working life. On Figure 4.1, the individual's
endowment point is point A. Show how much this
individual saves during his working life.

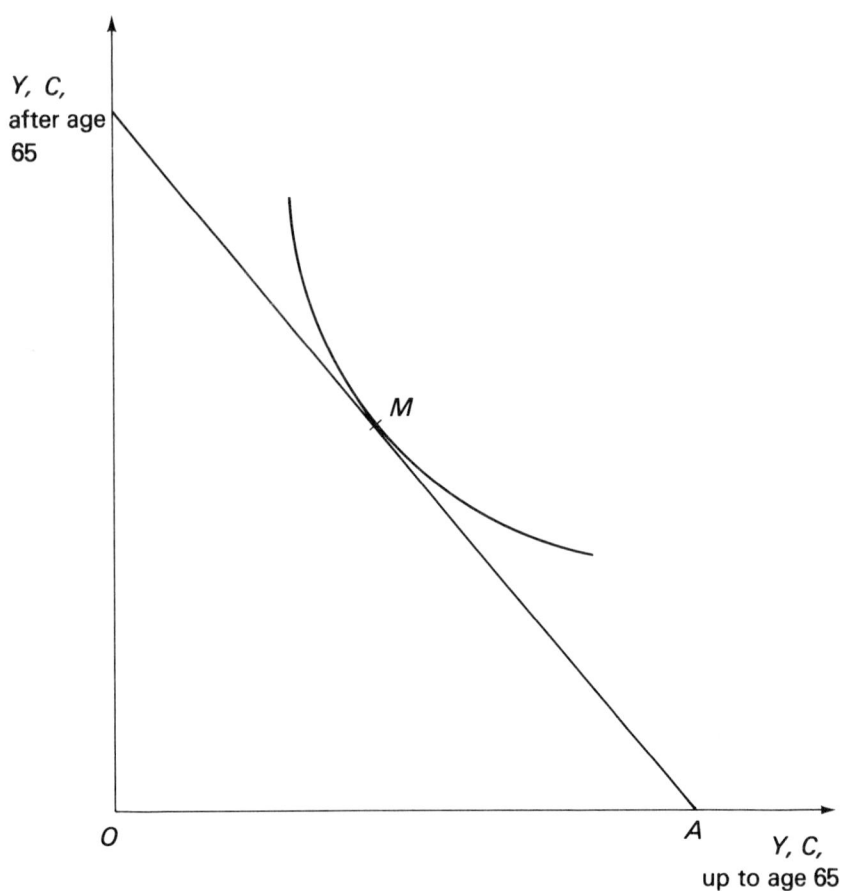

Figure 4.1

Question 8 We now introduce a social security scheme which requires the individual to pay social security contributions equal to $Y_1 Y_n$ leaving him with a net income of Y_n. As a result he receives a pension equal to Y_r on retirement. This is shown in Figure 4.2 below. What is this individual's endowment, given that he contributes to the social security scheme? Label this point B.

Question 9 What are his personal savings now (i.e. savings other than social security savings)? Have total savings changed?

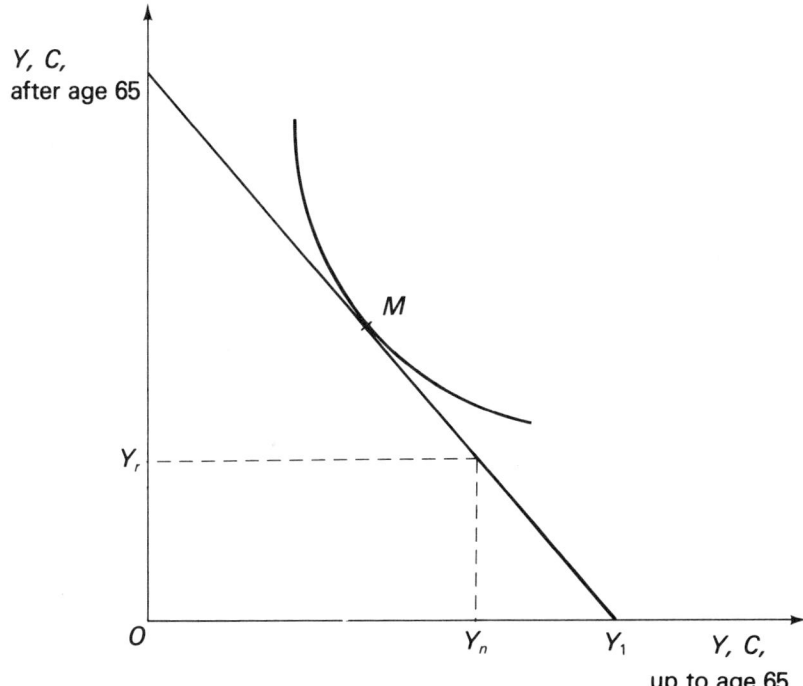

Figure 4.2

Question 10 Figure 4.2 represents an individual who saved during his
working life. Can you draw a similar diagram (using
Figure 4.3) for someone who saves nothing at all during
his working life, though his income is the same? What
must his indifference map look like? When social security
is introduced, can he still achieve the same level of
utility?

Question 11 Not everyone retires at the age of 65. If someone continues to work after 65, does this increase or decrease
the amount of savings required to finance retirement
consumption?

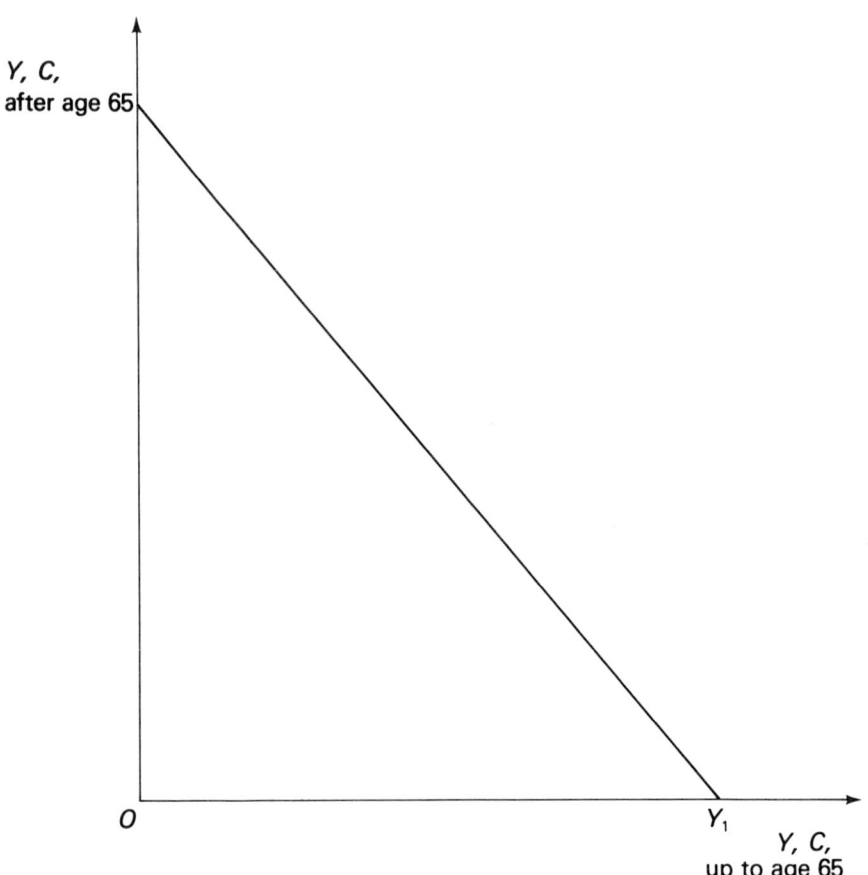

Figure 4.3

Question 12 If an individual were the sort of saver who aimed to save a set amount to cover retirement, would he have to save a larger or smaller proportion of his income up to retirement if he retires after the age of 65?

Question 13 Figure 4.2 has been redrawn below, as Figure 4.4. We now allow for the possibility that our individual continues to work after the age of 65. As a result he has some earned income in this period and his endowment point is shown as point D. If there were no social security scheme, what would he save up to the age of 65?

Question 14 Suppose now that social security is introduced and this individual decides to retire at 65, i.e. moves to point B. Compare his personal savings now with what they were when he was at point D. Have they fallen or risen?

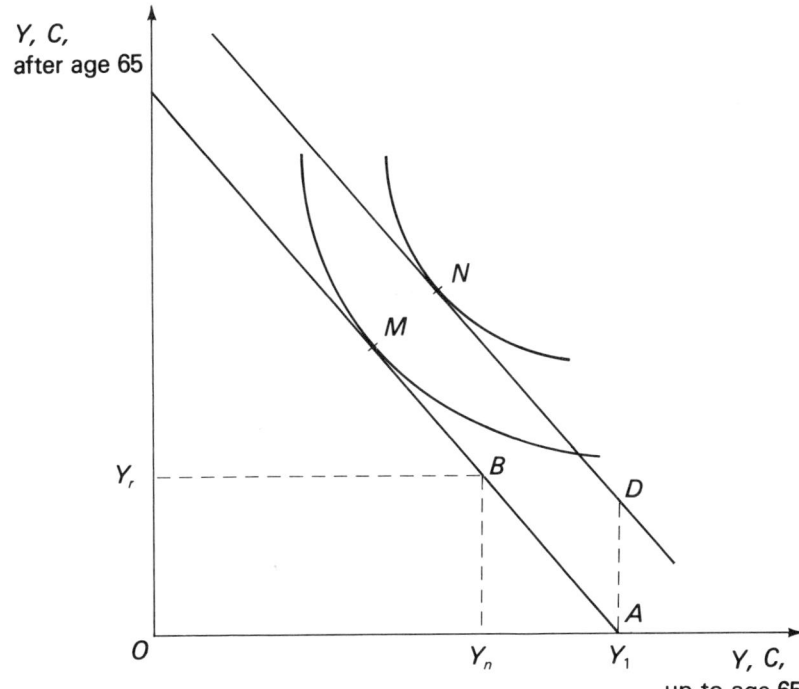

Figure 4.4

Question 15 If social security induces someone to retire earlier than they would otherwise have done, does this mean that personal savings will always change in the direction illustrated in Figure 4.4? On Figure 4.5 show that this need not be so.

Why may the introduction of social security induce people to retire earlier than they would otherwise have done? For most working people, participation in the state social security scheme is compulsory. However, while you must have made the necessary contributions to be eligible for a retirement

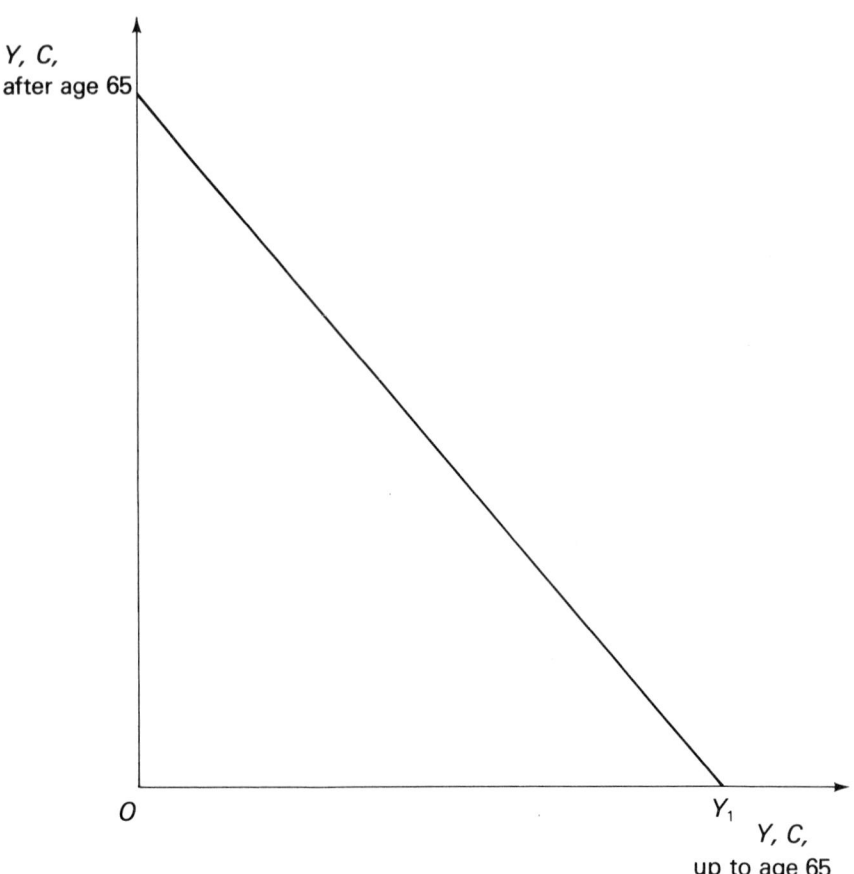

Figure 4.5

pension, you may not be able to draw your pension unless you retire because there are earnings restrictions. Earnings may be allowed up to certain levels but as earnings rise, you lose a larger and larger proportion of your pension until at a certain level you may no longer be eligible for any pension at all.

Question 16 In terms of such a person's labour—leisure choice, what would the constraint that he faces look like? Show this on Figure 4.6.

When there are earnings restrictions attached to the state pension, some people with high earnings may prefer to continue to work. However, when the state pension is equal to, or possibly larger than, a person's earnings after the age of 65, they will retire. (Can you see this from Figure 4.6? Show different wage rates and see if this affects the individual's optimal choice.)

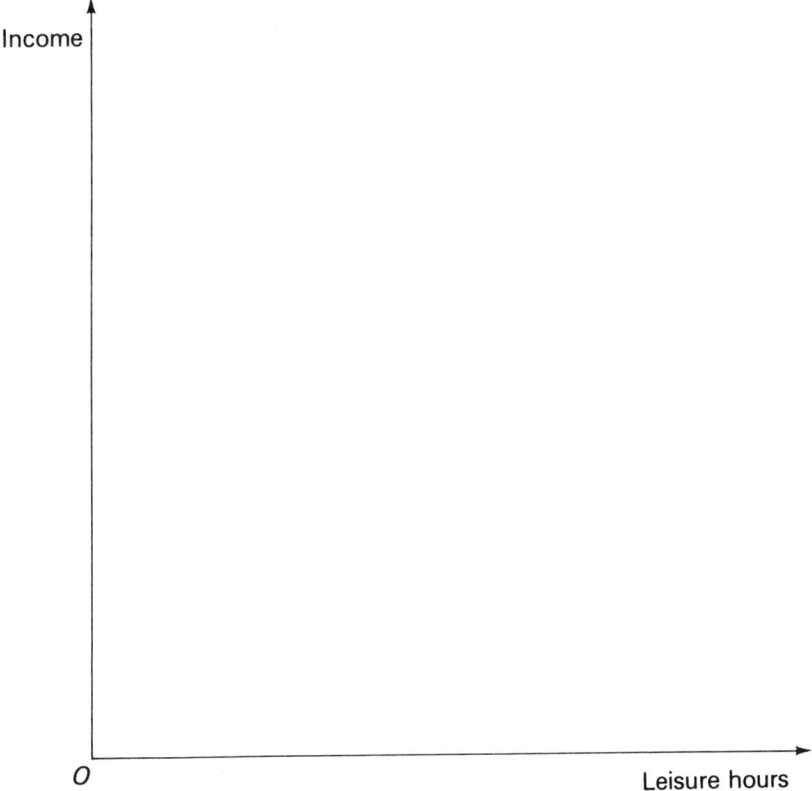

Figure 4.6

Question 17 We now go back to the diagram illustrated in Figure
4.4. This has been reproduced below as Figure 4.7. We
now assume that contributions to the state social security
scheme up to the official retirement age are compulsory.
A person's endowment at age 65, if he retires, is thus
point B. Now assume that potential earnings after the
age of 65 are equal to AD and assume further that the
state pension is only paid if earnings are zero. If this
person decided to continue working after 65, his
endowment point would therefore be point E. Make
sure you can see why this is so. If he were to continue
working, can he get to points M or N?

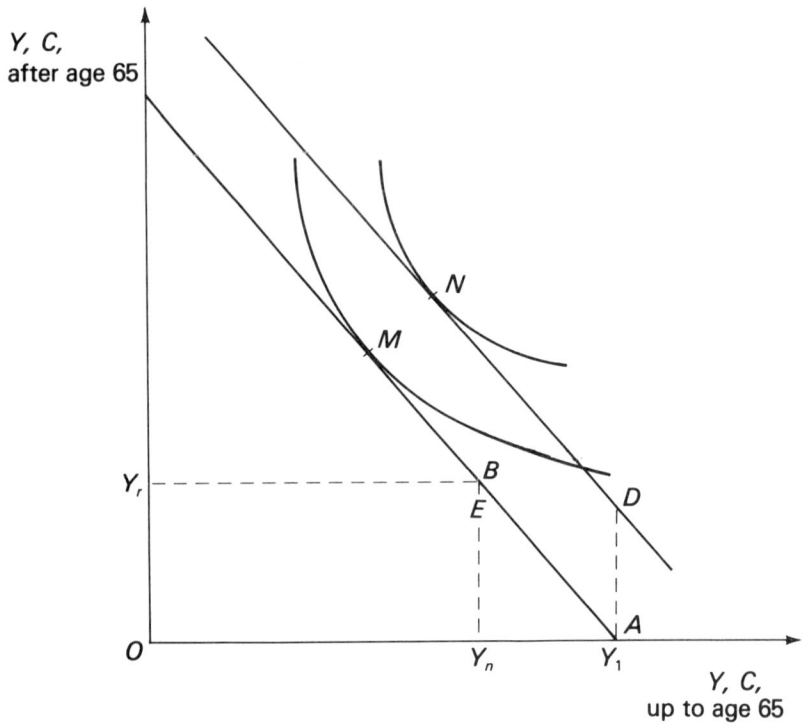

Figure 4.7

Feldstein's model has enabled us to analyse two effects arising from the introduction of social security:

(i) *The 'substitution' effect*: social security savings can be a substitute for personal savings. As you found in answering Questions 8 and 9, where an individual was saving before the introduction of the state social security scheme, the scheme will result in personal savings *falling*.

(ii) *The 'retirement' effect*: the introduction of social security may induce some people to retire earlier than they would otherwise have done. From your answers to Questions 13, 14 and 15, you know that personal savings may rise *or* fall.

Since the outcome of the retirement effect is ambiguous, it is not clear whether the *overall* effect (i.e. substitution plus retirement effects) of the introduction of social security is to lower or to raise personal saving. The only way to find out is to examine data on savings, i.e. undertake empirical analysis. In his article, Feldstein analyses savings data for the USA for the period from 1929 through to 1971 and he concludes that the introduction of social security reduced personal savings.[1]

His findings have aroused a certain amount of controversy and have led other people to undertake research in this area. If you are interested, you might like to look at some recent studies in Modigliani and Hemming (1983).

It is not the place here to go into these studies, but, instead, we will finish by asking why it should matter whether personal savings rise or fall with the advent of social security when total saving (i.e. personal saving plus social security saving) is unlikely to fall and indeed may rise, given that some people saved nothing at all when there was no compulsory state scheme. The British social security scheme is called the National Insurance Scheme, which suggests that it is a state insurance scheme run on similar lines to private insurance provided through the market. In private insurance schemes, an individual's contributions are invested by the insurance company to provide income from which the annuity will be paid in due course. The state scheme, however, is run on what are called 'pay as you go' lines. What this means is that current contributions by workers are paid out as pensions to current pensioners. When *you* eventually start to draw your old age pension, it will be the people who are working at that time who will be paying for your pension, as you paid for others when you worked. The state scheme thus redistributes income between age groups (or, in the case of unemployment benefits, from workers to unemployed) but the money is never channelled into funding investment as it is in private insurance. As all social security

1. Although there was an error in the calculations, this did not modify the main conclusions; see Feldstein 1982.

savings become transfer payments, the amount of savings available to finance investment falls with the introduction of a 'pay as you go' social security scheme and this will affect the growth rate of the economy, other things being equal. Put another way, by funding the state scheme in this way, we are trading off some growth against a redistribution of income. If the scheme had been funded as an insurance scheme, there would have been a longer interval before pensions could be paid, so an advantage of a 'pay as you go' scheme is that people can start to benefit much sooner. Another advantage is that contributions and pensions can rise in line with growth so that pensioners share in the rising standard of living.

Apart from the possible effects on the economy's growth rate, there is another aspect of the 'pay as you go' method of funding that we should consider. It is rather sensitive to changes in the age composition of the population. As today's workers finance today's pensioners, to keep a pensioner's standard of living constant (or to keep it in line with any rise in living standards) means that if the number of active workers declines, the burden on remaining workers will increase. If the number of workers remains constant but there is an increase in the number of pensioners, again the burden on workers will increase unless the increased expenditure can be financed out of economic growth.

Question 18 The estimated average number of people who received retirement pensions in 1983—4 was 9,180,000 (*The Government's Expenditure Plans 1984—5 to 1986—7*, 1984). Some population projections are given in Table 4.1. Under what conditions do you consider it likely to

Table 4.1 Population Projections (000's)

Age group	1981	1991	2001	2011	2021	2031	2041
Working age	33,728	34,393	34,558	35,143	34,830	33,781	34,469
Pensionable age & over[a]	9,845	10,258	10,052	10,687	11,721	13,120	12,761
Numbers of working age per pensioner	3.426	3.353	3.438	3.288	2.972	2.557	2.701

Source: OPCS 1983.
Note: (a) Pensionable age of 60 for women, 65 for men.

be politically feasible to maintain the real value of
retirement pensions? In 2029, when you will probably
have retired, do these projections suggest that your state
retirement pension will keep you in the style of living to
which you hope to become accustomed?

References

*Feldstein, M.S. (1974) 'Social security, induced retirement, and the aggregate
   capital accumulation', *Journal of Political Economy*, 82, pp. 905–926.
Feldstein, M.S. (1982) 'Social security and private saving: a reply', *Journal of
   Political Economy*, 90, pp. 630–642.
Modigliani, F. and Hemming, R. (eds.) (1983) *The Determinants of National Saving
   and Wealth*, Proceedings of a Conference held by the International Economics
   Association, Macmillan.

The Government's Expenditure Plans 1984–5 to 1986–7 (1984), Cmnd. 9143,
   HMSO.
OPCS (1983) *OPCS Monitor*, 8 March.
Royal Commission on the Distribution of Income and Wealth (1978), Layard, R.
   et al., Background Paper No. 5, *The Causes of Poverty*, HMSO.

---

* Suggested supplementary reading.

5

The Risky Business of Investing in Supertankers

Life is uncertain. As we saw in Problems 3 and 4, you do not know whether you will fall ill or whether you will experience unemployment at some period in your life. You will frequently have to make choices when you are not sure what the outcome will be and we now wish to extend our consumer theory to encompass such situations. How do people choose when faced with risk? Von Neumann and Morgenstern (1944) developed a set of axioms from which they deduced that the rational consumer will maximise expected utility. What this means is that it is hypothesised that an individual will rank alternative prospects according to the expected utility such prospects provide.[1]

By examining whether an individual is indifferent between a certain and an uncertain prospect, by assigning utility numbers to the outcomes of the uncertain prospect, and by varying either the probability of these outcomes or the value of the certain prospect, it is possible to plot a species of cardinal utility function for that individual. This von Neumann—Morgenstern utility function can then be used to show that, where the function exhibits diminishing marginal utility of income, the person is risk averse and he or she will be willing to pay to avoid risk. Problem 5 asks you to choose between a certain prospect and a simple gamble, and shows you how your answers can be used to reveal your attitude towards risk. Most of the problem only requires that you answer some questions about how much you would be willing to pay for a lottery ticket. Nevertheless, to get as much as possible out of the problem, it would be a good idea to make sure you understand the following:

---

1. The debate continues over the principles that underlie any theory of rational behaviour under uncertainty. Expected utility maximisation is one hypothesis that has proved very useful in analysing various situations but there are other approaches. If you are interested, you might like to follow up the prospect theory of Kahneman and Tversky (1979).

(a) the difference between expected utility and
   expected value;
(b) the difference between ordinal and cardinal utility;
(c) what is meant by a 'fair gamble'.

At the beginning of 1972, before the first oil price rise, shipowners transporting oil faced a healthy and profitable market. Over ten years later, the recession had brought a large fall in the demand for oil so that shipowners faced severe financial problems with many tankers laid up or operating at less than optimal capacity. Investing in shipping is not only an extremely costly business but also a very risky one.

Many supertankers are owned by oil companies but you can see from Table 5.1 that independent shipowners hold the larger proportion. Table 5.2 shows the percentage of inactive tankers in recent years.

Any shipowner considering investing in additional vessels has to make a choice between:

(i) type of vessel, e.g. tanker, liner, container, carrier
   (ore, gas or chemical), etc;
(ii) size of vessel.

Some types of trade are more profitable than others: the expected return is higher for tankers than for liners. However, some trades are more risky than others; freight rates can fluctuate more frequently and more widely for tankers than liners. In general, larger vessels are more economical to operate than smaller ones. The shipowner, therefore, has to decide whether to invest a given sum in, say, one supertanker or two smaller vessels. While the expected rate of return would be higher from the supertanker, it will be less risky to invest in two smaller vessels as freight rates for vessels are not perfectly positively correlated.

Peter Lorange and Victor Norman (1973) noted that independent Scandinavian shipowners had invested relatively heavily in larger, rather than smaller, oil tankers and they decided to study the shipowners' risk preferences. In order to do this they assumed that Scandinavian shipowners acted in accordance with the von Neumann—Morgenstern axioms for choice under uncertainty. In other words, they sought to derive the von Neumann—Morgenstern (NM) utility functions of these shipowners. How did they do this? The best way to understand how they went about their research is to try out their approach on yourself.

Question 1   Suppose I offered you a lottery ticket where the outcomes are such that you either win 5 pence or 50 pence and that the probability (P) of you receiving 5 pence is one-half. At what price would you be indifferent between buying the lottery ticket and not buying?

Table 5.1 Tanker Fleet Ownership by Vessel Size

Ship size (dwt)	End 1973			End 1977			End 1982		
	Oil Co.'s	Independents	Total	Oil Co.'s	Independents	Total	Oil Co.'s	Independents	Total
10– 49,999	973	1,099	2,072	844	691	1,535	732	575	1,307
50–174,999	258	585	843	361	695	1,056	348	683	1,031
175–300,000+	125	255	380	284	454	738	239	398	637
Total	1,356	1,939	3,295	1,489	1,840	3,329	1,319	1,656	2,975

Table 5.2 Tankers Laid-Up by Vessel Size

Ship size (dwt)	End 1977						End 1982					
	Oil Co.'s		Independents		Total		Oil Co.'s		Independents		Total	
	No.	% of fleet	No.	% of fleet	No.	% of fleet	No.	% of fleet	No.	% of fleet	No.	% of fleet
10– 49,999	25	3	100	14	125	8	17	2	67	11	84	6
50–174,999	20	6	94	14	114	11	18	5	107	11	125	12
175–300,000+	6	2	66	15	72	10	45	19	155	39	200	31
Total	51	3	260	14	311	9	80	6	329	20	409	14

Source: H.P. Drewry (Shipping Consultants) Ltd. (1978); and personal communication.

The price you gave in answer to Question 1 is what we will call the 'certainty equivalent': at this price you are indifferent between having that amount of money for *certain* (i.e. you do not buy the lottery ticket) and buying the ticket.

Question 2 Make a note of this price on Table 5.3 below in the column headed 'certainty equivalent' (z), in the space for Choice 1. (Ignore the column headed NM utility for the moment.)

Now consider Choice 2 in Table 5.3: suppose this represents a lottery ticket where the outcomes are that you either win 5 pence or the amount that you were prepared to pay for the lottery ticket of Choice 1. Say, for example, that in answer to Question 1 you had said that your 'certainty equivalent' was 30 pence, then in Choice 2 you are being asked at what price you would be indifferent between buying a lottery ticket where you have a fifty—fifty chance of winning 5 or 30 pence, or not buying the ticket at all.

Question 3 Fill in the certainty equivalents for Choices 2 to 7 inclusive on Table 5.3.

We must now fill in the column headed 'NM utility' in Table 5.3. Consider Choice 1 again: let us assume that your certainty equivalent for this choice

Table 5.3

Choice no.	Bad outcome: Payoff	P	Good outcome: Payoff	P	Certainty equivalent z	NM utility U(z)
1	5	0.5	50	0.5	—	—
2	5	0.5	CE_1	0.5	—	—
3	CE_2	0.5	CE_1	0.5	—	—
4	5	0.5	CE_2	0.5	—	—
5	CE_1	0.5	50	0.5	—	—
6	CE_5	0.5	50	0.5	—	—
7	CE_1	0.5	CE_5	0.5	—	—

Note: CE = certainty equivalent

was 30 pence. Then you are indifferent between buying the ticket at 30 pence and not buying it. The outcomes for Choice 1 are:

Worst outcome (x_0) = 5 pence

and

Best outcome (x_1) = 50 pence

and the probability (P) of x_0 is one-half. If you are indifferent between paying an amount of 30 pence (z_1) for the lottery ticket and not buying the ticket, thus keeping the 30 pence, this must mean that:

$$U(z_1) = P \cdot U(x_0) + (1-P) \cdot U(x_1)$$

or

$$U(30) = \tfrac{1}{2} \cdot U(5) + \tfrac{1}{2} \cdot U(50)$$

We now want the NM utility index for this certainty equivalent. To obtain this, we assign numbers representing the utility of 5 and 50 pence. We can assign any numbers we like, providing that the number we pick for $U(50)$ is greater than that for $U(5)$ as the NM utility function is unique up to a linear transformation.

Question 4 What does 'unique up to a linear transformation' mean?

Suppose we set $U(5)$ equal to 2 and $U(50)$ equal to 36. The NM utility index for $U(30)$ is found as follows:

$$U(z_1) = \tfrac{1}{2} \cdot (2) + \tfrac{1}{2} \cdot (36) = 19$$

You can now enter the figure 19 in the NM utility column for Choice 1.

We can now extend the index: for example, we could make use of the figure we have entered for Choice 1.

$$U(z_0) = \tfrac{1}{2} \cdot U(x_1) + \tfrac{1}{2} \cdot U(z_1) = 27.5$$

(Work this out for yourself and make sure you understand what is going on.)

Question 5 You can now complete the NM utility column for each of the 7 Choices set out in Table 5.3. When you have done this, plot your results on Figure 5.1, using the figures you have filled in for the certainty equivalent and the NM utility columns. What you have plotted is *your* NM utility function. What does it look like? Does it exhibit diminishing, constant or increasing marginal utility of wealth? What does it suggest about your attitude to risk?

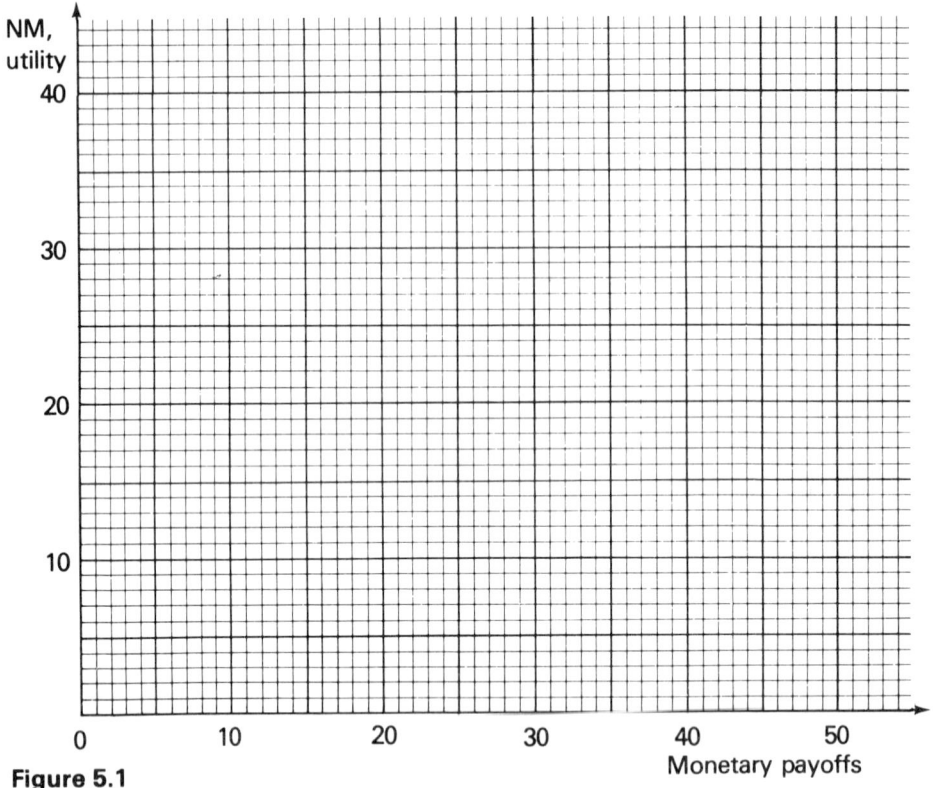

Figure 5.1

(a) Owner *A*'s risk-preference curves. This decision maker is risk prone under conditions of good liquidity (solid line), but risk averse under conditions of weak liquidity (dotted line).

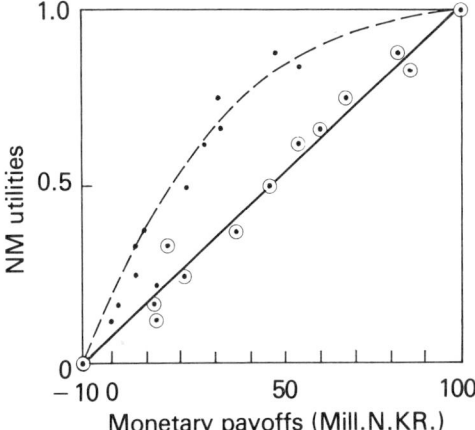

(b) Owner *B*'s risk-preference curves. This decision maker is close to risk neutral under conditions of good liquidity (solid line), but quite risk averse under conditions of weak liquidity (dotted line).

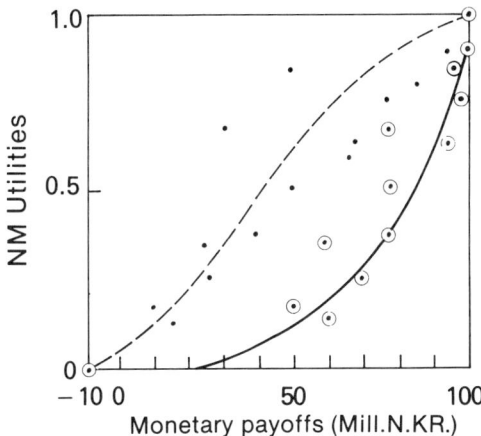

(c) Owner *C*'s risk-preference curves. This decision maker is rather inconsistent in his answers, as indicated by the large spread of the observations. He appears to be fairly risk prone under good liquidity conditions (solid line), and close to risk neutral under weak liquidity conditions (dotted line).

Source: Lorange and Norman (1973).

Figure 5.2

Question 6 To make quite sure that you have fully understood the
meaning of 'unique up to a linear transformation', you
might like to work out the NM utility index choosing to
assign different values to $U(x_0)$ and $U(x_1)$ and check
whether your NM utility function still shows the same
attitude to risk.

Now compare your utility index with those that Lorange and Norman
obtained for their shipowners. They put the same choices as you have made
to the shipowners, except that the outcomes were in millions of Norwegian
Krona (at that time a new 220,000 dwt supertanker cost about 220 million
NKr.). They asked them for their certainty equivalents under two different
states of the world: in one case the shipowner was asked to imagine he faced
a satisfactory liquidity position (as he was indeed currently experiencing
with the buoyant freight market) and in the other an unsatisfactory one.
Lorange and Norman found that out of the 17 owners they interviewed, the
indices fell into three groups illustrated by Figure 5.2, (a), (b) and (c), which
has been reproduced from Lorange and Norman's article, with their
comments.

Lorange and Norman concluded that when the liquidity of the shipowner
was good, the owner was a risk taker. To quote them:

> We found the shipowners to be risk prone only when their
> liquidity position was sufficiently good to enable them to bear
> the potential loss from accepting an unfair gamble. In other
> words, they were willing to accept unfair gambles with a
> (small) chance to gain considerably, provided such gambles
> did not endanger their future operations. (1973, p. 59)

At that time no-one foresaw the oil crisis of 1973 but by December 1977 a
Norwegian Shipowners' Association reported that 'some 60 Norwegian shipping companies, owning some 30 per cent of the country's tonnage, will be in
serious financial difficulties in 1979 if freight rates do not improve' (Drewry
1978, p. 10).

Question 7 What is an 'unfair gamble'?

The type of risk we have been discussing has been risk arising from the
variability of returns on investment. Shipowners face another type of risk:
the possible loss or damage of the vessel due to fire, explosion, collision, bad
weather, etc. This type of risk can be insured against.

Question 8 Why can't shipowners insure against variable returns on
investment?

Question 9 Given the attitudes to risk illustrated above, would you expect the shipowners to take out insurance against damage or loss of the vessel? To the best of your knowledge, do shipowners generally insure against such risks?

Question 10 Why will a risk-averse person not take a fair gamble, while a risk-preferrer will?

Question 11 In 1983 there was a very large fire at the biggest army store in Britain. The store and its contents had to be completely written off; nothing had been insured. Do you think that this indicates that the government is a risk taker or can you think of another explanation why the government did not take out insurance on the market?

References

H.P. Drewry (Shipping Consultants) Ltd. (1978), *World Shipping Statistics 1977*.

Kahneman, Daniel and Tversky, Amos (1979) 'Prospect theory: an analysis of decision under risk', *Econometrica*, 47, pp. 263–291.

* Lorange, Peter and Norman, Victor N. (1973) 'Risk preferences in Scandinavian shipping', *Applied Economics*, 5, pp. 49–59.

von Neumann, John and Morgenstern, Oskar (1944) *Theory of Games and Economic Behaviour*, Princeton.

* Suggested supplementary reading.

6

Crime and Punishment

You may be surprised to find a problem about burglars in a book on applied economics. Gary Becker has applied economic theory to many aspects of human life outside of the range of problems usually analysed by economists. In a wide-ranging article on crime (Becker 1968) he suggests that the decision whether or not to commit an illegal act can be analysed by the theory of consumer choice and, given the risky nature of crime, the appropriate model is that of expected utility maximisation. Becker suggests that criminals are risk takers and it is this hypothesis we examine in this problem. Before tackling the problem, check that you understand:

(a) expected utility maximisation;
(b) why individuals who are characterised by an increasing marginal utility of income are risk takers; and
(c) why individuals with diminishing marginal utility of income are risk averse.

In 1983, 3,247,000 notifiable offences were recorded by the police for England and Wales; 813,386 of these were for burglary and robbery and the value of the property stolen was estimated to be £304,267,000 (*Criminal Statistics England and Wales* 1983, 1984). The figure for the number of burglaries is probably an underestimate as other sources suggest that twice as many domestic offences are committed than are recorded (op. cit., Table 2A). Burglary would seem to be a profitable business, but is it really so? The value realised by burglars would be less than the total reported value: a small amount (about 6½ per cent) was recovered while, of the remainder, much was in goods rather than money and the burglars would be unlikely to be able to dispose of these at their full value. The rewards for burglary would thus be considerably less than the full value recorded as stolen. Against the rewards have to be set the costs. If the burglar is not caught, his costs are small, but if caught and convicted, at best there would be a fine while at worst there would be loss of liberty and earnings (or unemployment benefit)

51

while in prison. The detection rate for burglaries is quite low — about 30 per cent of all such offences were cleared up in 1983 (op. cit.).

Two economists at Nottingham University studied burglaries in one district of Nottingham in 1973 and concluded that burglary did not pay; indeed, they calculated that the average net loss per burglary in this district amounted to £59.30 (Lees and Chiplin 1975). Their study raises the question as to why burglars in Nottingham burgle if returns are so poor. Gary Becker (1968) has suggested that criminals are risk takers. If this were so, it would provide an explanation since people who prefer risk will take on an unfair bet. In this exercise we examine how Becker arrived at this conclusion about criminal behaviour.

Starting from the proposition that crime is a business activity undertaken for much the same reasons as other activities, Becker argues that a potential offender, after weighing up the benefits and costs, will choose that activity which maximises his expected utility. If a person chooses illegal activity, it is because his estimate of the benefits and costs, together with his subjective probability of getting caught, differs from other people's. According to Becker, the number of offences a person commits depends on the probability of conviction, punishment if convicted and other variables such as income available from other activities (legal and illegal), willingness to commit an illegal act, etc.

Since an illegal act, such as burglary, is risky, an individual will be maximising *expected* utility, and Becker (1968, p. 177) defines the potential burglar's choice problem as follows:

$$EU = P \cdot U(Y-f) + (1-P) \cdot U(Y) \qquad (1)$$

where EU is an individual's expected utility; P is the probability of conviction; Y is income, monetary plus psychic, from an offence; and f is monetary equivalent of punishment if convicted.

Now, if the probability of conviction increases — for example, more policemen are recruited and patrols are more frequent — expected utility should fall. A similar result should follow if punishment is more severe.

Question 1 Check this by differentiating equation (1) with respect to P and f:

$$\frac{\partial EU}{\partial P} = \qquad\qquad\qquad (2)$$

$$\frac{\partial EU}{\partial f} = \qquad\qquad\qquad (3)$$

(*Hint*: to find $\dfrac{\partial EU}{\partial f}$ use the chain rule.)

As we have already mentioned, Becker concludes that criminals are risk takers.

> The widespread generalization that offenders are more deter-
> red by the probability of conviction than by the punishment
> when convicted turns out to imply in the expected-utility
> approach that offenders are risk preferrers, at least in the rele-
> vant region of punishments. (Becker, op. cit., p. 178)

In order to understand how Becker reaches this conclusion we start by examining carefully what he says about criminal behaviour.

> It is easily shown that an increase in [the probability of con-
> viction] would reduce the expected utility, and thus the
> number of offenses, more than an equal percentage increase in
> [punishment] if [the offender] has preference for risk; the
> increase in [punishment] would have the greater effect if he
> has aversion to risk; and they would have the same effect if he
> is risk neutral. (loc. cit.)

From this passage we see that Becker assesses the deterrent effects of being caught and of punishment in terms of *elasticities*. Remember that offences are a function of EU. If the elasticity of offences with respect to the probability of conviction (E_p) is:

$$E_p = \frac{-\partial EU \cdot P}{\partial P \cdot EU} \tag{4}$$

while that of offences with respect to punishment (E_f) is:

$$E_f = \frac{-\partial EU \cdot f}{\partial f \cdot EU} \tag{5}$$

and offenders are more deterred by the probability of conviction than by punishment, then according to Becker, $E_p > E_f$ implies that criminals are risk takers.

We start by examining the case where an individual is risk averse: according to Becker we should find $E_p < E_f$.

Question 2 We begin to answer this question by writing out these elasticities (equations (4) and (5)), substituting from the optimality conditions given in equations (2) and (3) above.

$$E_p = \tag{6}$$

$$E_f = \tag{7}$$

Question 3   Now $E_p \gtreqqless E_f$

$$\text{as } \frac{U(Y) - U(Y-f)}{f} \gtreqqless \frac{U'(Y-f)}{\quad} \tag{8}$$

Show how (8) is derived from equations (6) and (7).

While we expect an individual's marginal utility of income to be positive, we do not know whether marginal utility is diminishing, constant or increasing, i.e.

$$U' > 0, \qquad U'' \gtreqqless 0$$

Question 4   (a) If a person is risk averse, what is the sign of U''?
(b) And if a person is a risk taker?

Question 5   In Figure 6.1 the case of an individual with diminishing marginal utility of income is shown. On the utility axis, label $U(Y)$ and $U(Y-f)$. What is $U'(Y-f)$?

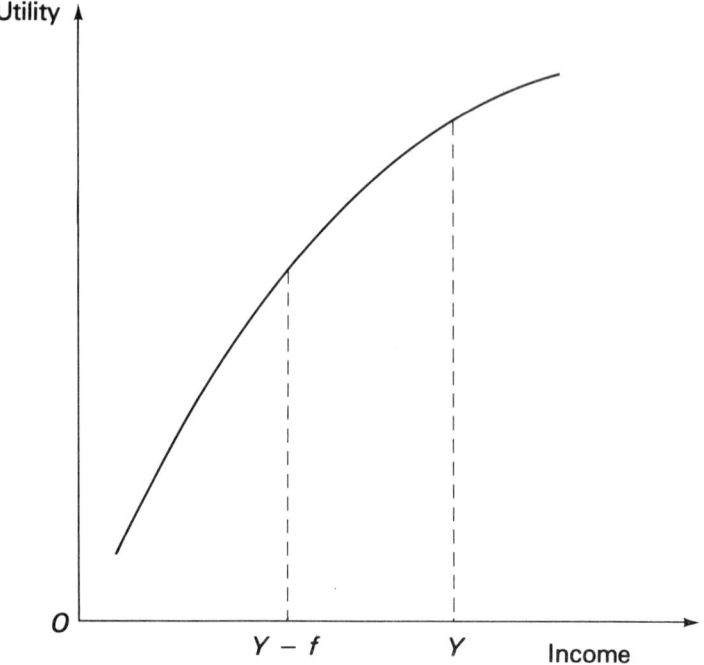

Figure 6.1

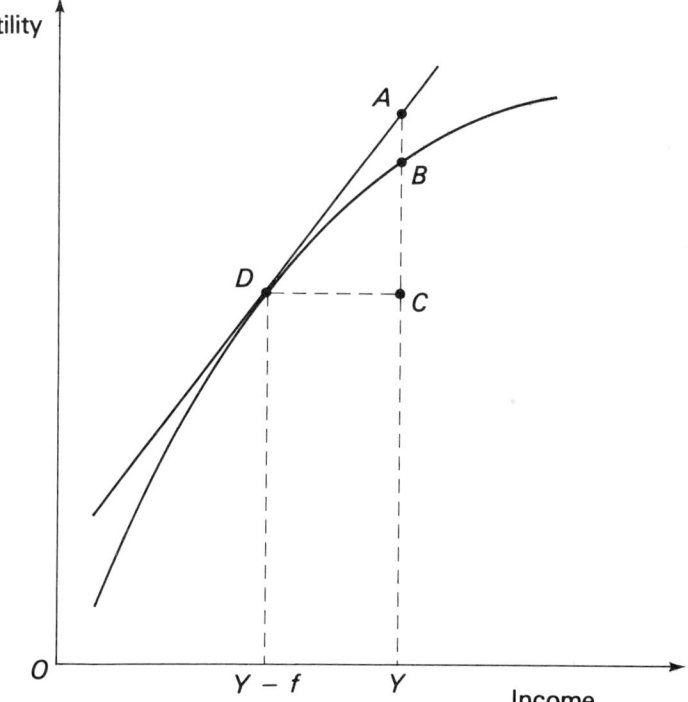

Figure 6.2

Figure 6.1 has been reproduced in Figure 6.2 but a line has been drawn tangent to the utility function at point D. Using the letters in the diagram, the right-hand side of equation (8) is:

$$U'(Y-f) = \frac{AC}{DC}$$

Question 7 Now it is your turn; using the letters, find:

    (a) $U(Y) - U(Y-f) =$

    (b) $f =$

    (c) $\dfrac{U(Y) - U(Y-f)}{f} =$

    (c) is, of course, the left-hand side of equation (8).

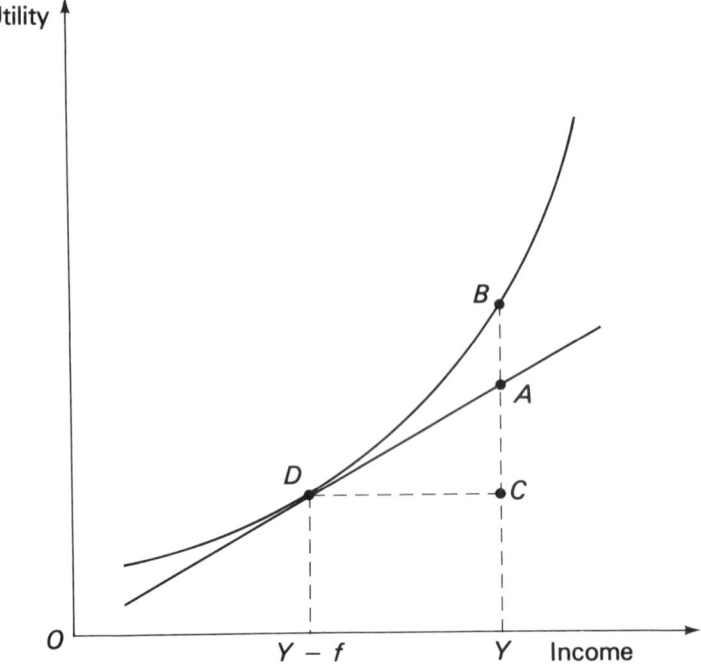

Figure 6.3

Question 8 You can now work out whether

$$\frac{U(Y) - U(Y-f)}{f} \geq U'(Y-f)$$

and thus whether $E_p \geq E_f$. What do you conclude?

This completes the analysis for a risk-averse individual and we now repeat it for the case of a risk-preferrer. Figure 6.3 illustrates this case.

Question 9 (a) Find

$$\frac{U(Y) - U(Y-f)}{f}$$

(b) Find $U'(Y-f)$
(c) In this case, is $E_p > E_f$? Compare your answer with that to Question 8.

We have now seen how Becker reached his conclusion that criminals are risk takers. However, there are some questions we should ask about the way he formulates the criminal prospect in equation (1) and how punishment is defined.

The successful outcome is not problematical: if a criminal completes a job and gets away with it, then his current wealth (W) is augmented by the amount of his gain (G). The best outcome can thus be written as $U(W+G)$. What about the worst outcome? There are various possibilities: some criminals not only make off with their loot but also manage to hide it away so that even if they are caught and convicted, they do not forfeit their illgotten gains. Others may lose part and some may even lose it all if they are caught and convicted. Some might even get caught in the act and never lay their hands on the goods at all. One way to write the worst outcome so that it encompasses all these possibilities is to write it as:

$$U(W+G-(1-x)G-L)$$

where $0 \leqslant x \leqslant 1$ and x is the proportion of the haul that the criminal retains; and L represents the costs, in the form of a fine or the monetary equivalent of imprisonment, of being caught and convicted.

Question 10 Write out the criminal prospect with the outcomes as specified above.

$$EU = \tag{9}$$

Question 11 (a) If $x = 0$, what is the worst prospect facing the offender?
(b) If $x = 1$, what difference will it make?

Now, remember that Becker drew his conclusions by comparing the *elasticities* of offences with respect to probability of conviction and that of punishment. E_p raises no problems but E_f requires a clear definition of punishment. It has been argued that punishment deters people from committing illegal acts; but how do we measure the punishment the burglar faces if caught? Precisely what is the 'punishment' that deters burglars? Is it the fine/prison sentence? Or is it either of these *plus* the loss of part or all of the loot from the burglary? In other words, is the relevant elasticity, E_f, to be defined as $f = L$ (the fine or the monetary equivalent of a prison sentence) or as $f = (1-x)G+L$ (where x is the proportion of the gain retained by the criminal)? It would not matter which definition we use if they both gave the same result, but they do not (see Brown and Reynolds 1973, Heineke 1975). In order to see what difference the choice of definition makes, we work through the case of a risk-averse individual, considering two possibilities: $x=0$ and $x=1$.

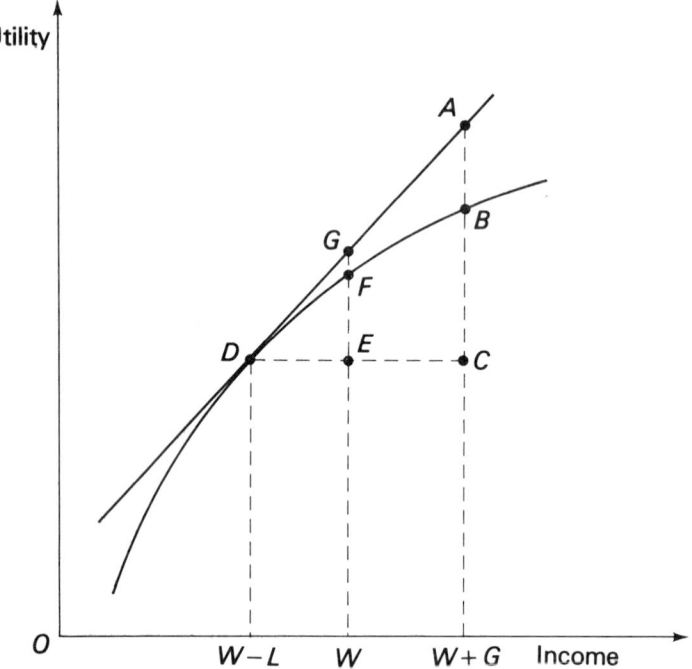

Figure 6.4

Question 12 (a) When $x = 0$, write out the criminal's prospect:

$EU =$

(b) Use Figure 6.4 and find whether $E_p \gtrless E_f$ when $f = L$.

(c) Repeat taking the case where $f = (1-x)G+L$ (remember $x = 0$).

Are the results the same for (b) and (c) and are they consistent with Becker's hypothesis?

Question 13 Now repeat the procedure in Question 12 but this time take $x = 1$ and use Figure 6.5 (you will need to add something to the diagram).

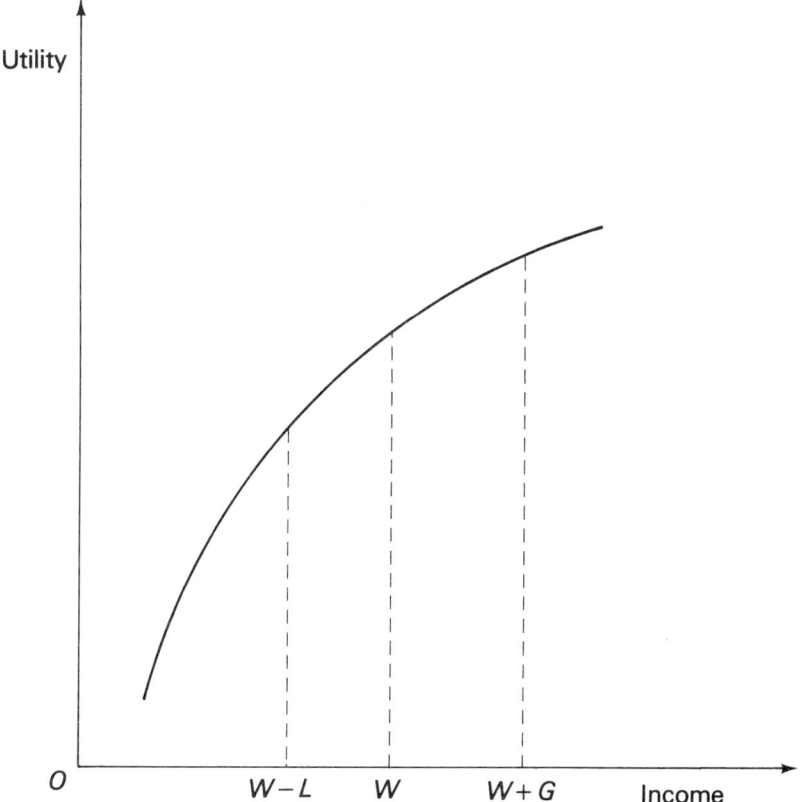

Figure 6.5

Question 14 Does Becker's hypothesis about criminal behaviour always hold when punishment refers only to the fine or prison sentence, that is to say when $f = L$? Does it make any difference if punishment is defined so as to include the possible loss of illegal gains, i.e. $f = (1-x)G+L$?

Question 15 Which do you think is the more appropriate definition?

It is certainly not unusual for some criminals to retain a substantial proportion of their illegal gains, even if caught and convicted. *The Times* reported on 12 May 1984 that the Government is planning to introduce legislation which would permit the seizure of assets from criminals who have legally invested the proceeds of their crime in property or shares. The main target of the proposed legislation is drug-dealers.

As you now understand, Becker's hypothesis that criminals are risk takers only holds in certain circumstances. Nevertheless, I would not wish to leave you with the conclusion that economic analysis cannot be usefully applied to the study of criminal behaviour. The hypothesis about criminal attitudes to risk is only a small footnote in Becker's article on crime and punishment and, if you are interested in the topic, you may like to look at the rest of his article. You may also be interested to learn how Becker has used economic theory to analyse various aspects of family life. He has written on the incidence of polygyny, polyandry and monogamy in efficient marriage 'markets', on the determinants of marital instability, on the demand for children (both quantity and quality) and on many other topics. His work on the allocation of time within the household has inspired a great deal of research. If you would like to read some of Becker's work, I suggest that you start by looking at *The Economic Approach to Human Behavior* (1976) or *A Treatise on the Family* (1981).

References

Becker, G. (1968) 'Crime and punishment: an economic approach', *Journal of Political Economy*, **76**, pp. 169–217.

Becker, G. (1976) *The Economic Approach to Human Behavior*, University of Chicago Press.

Becker, G. (1981) *A Treatise on the Family*, Harvard University Press.

*Brown, W.W. and Reynolds, M.O. (1973) 'Crime and "punishment": risk implications', *Journal of Economic Theory*, **6**, pp. 508–514.

*Heineke, J.M. (1975) 'A note on modeling the criminal choice problem', *Journal of Economic Theory*, **10**, pp. 113–116.

Lees, D. and Chiplin, B. (1975) 'Does crime pay?', *Lloyds Bank Review*, No. 116, pp. 30–39.

Criminal Statistics England and Wales 1983 (1984), Cmnd. 9349, HMSO.

---

* Suggested supplementary reading.

7

Famine in Bengal

How is it possible for people to die from starvation when there is no shortage of food in their country? This is the question we consider here where we look at an economy in disequilibrium. Very often in analysis we focus on one market and examine the demand and supply relationships for that market. In this example it is important to note how markets are linked and how changes in one can affect transactions in another. With the Edgeworth—Bowley box we can show that voluntary trade is mutually beneficial. However, just how well off you will be after trading depends not only on what you have to offer but also on what you want to buy and their relative prices.

Before you start the problem, be sure you understand:

(a) *the Edgeworth—Bowley trading box;*
(b) *the region of mutual advantage;*
(c) *the Edgeworth contract curve;*
(d) *budget lines and competitive equilibrium;*
(e) *cross-price elasticity of demand.*

In 1943 there was a terrible famine in Bengal. The rural areas suffered most: estimates of the number who died from starvation and the subsequent epidemics vary from 1½ million (the official Famine Inquiry Commission) to 3 million (Sen 1977).

The official explanation was that there was a shortage of rice, the main staple crop. Amartya Sen, however, offers an alternative explanation (Sen, op. cit.). Before we consider this, let us first consider how we could test the validity of the official explanation.

Question 1 What information would you need to evaluate a view that the cause of the famine was insufficiency of food grains to feed the population of Bengal? Before you go

61

on to the next section, write down the sort of information you would need and note any adjustments or
calculations you would perform.
(*Hint*: is the amount produced in a country at any period of
time equal to the amount available in the market?)

Although there are three harvests a year in Bengal, 73 per cent of the total
rice crop is gathered at the winter harvest in November and December. Taking December 1941 as the base period, Sen found that one year later the
wholesale price index for rice had risen to 188 and by 20 August 1943 it was
498 (Sen, op. cit., Table 1). Price rises are, of course, what you would expect
if there were a sudden large fall in supply. Sen's findings on the availability
of food grains are reproduced in Table 7.1.

Question 2 Study this table carefully and compare the figures for
1943 (the famine year) with those for 1941 (a year when
there was no famine). How well do these figures support the official explanation?

It would seem that the official explanation does not fit the facts as set out
in Table 7.1. Nevertheless, people were dying from starvation. How can this
be explained?

Sen's explanation hinges on the concept of 'exchange entitlement'. He
writes:

> In an exchange economy, . . . the *terms* of exchange constitute
> a factor of some importance of its own, and a family's ability
> to buy food depends on the rates at which its labour and com-
> modity possessions can be exchanged into food. (Sen, op. cit.,
> p. 34)

Question 3 What is an exchange economy? Can you think of an
example of an economy which is not an exchange
economy?

Question 4 To understand the quotation from Sen, we start by considering a very simple economy in which families produce fish and/or rice and we concentrate on two
families. In any period these two families will produce a
given amount of rice and fish. Draw an Edgeworth-
Bowley box (as Figure 7.1) to illustrate this. (Will the
box be square?) Use page 64 for your diagram.

Table 7.1 Availability of Food Grains in Bengal 1938–43 (unit = 1 million tons, for columns (2)–(7); 1941 value = 100 for (8) and (9))

(1) Period	(2) Output of rice (official estimates)	(3) Net imports of rice (official estimates)	(4) Current supply of rice (official)	(5) Adjusted output of rice	(6) Adjusted current supply of rice	(7) Rice & wheat: adjusted current supply	(8) Index of total food grains supply	(9) Index of per capita food grains availability
I. Annual data								
1938	8.474	0.033	8.507	9.848	9.981	10.217	123	127
1939	7.922	0.382	8.304	9.114	9.596	9.787	118	120
1940	8.223	0.258	8.481	9.524	9.882	10.196	122	123
1941	6.768	0.223	6.991	7.631	7.954	8.332	100	100
1942	9.296	−0.102	9.194	10.776	10.774	10.947	131	130
1943	7.628	0.264	7.892	8.632	8.896	9.235	111	109
II. Moving averages: 2 years								
1938–39			8.406		9.789	10.002	120	123
1939–40			8.393		9.739	9.992	120	122
1940–41			7.736		8.918	9.264	111	112
1941–42			8.093		9.364	9.640	116	115
1942–43			8.543		9.835	10.091	121	119
III. Moving averages: 3 years								
1938–40			8.431		9.820	10.067	121	123
1939–41			7.925		9.144	9.438	113	114
1940–42			8.222		9.537	9.825	118	118
1941–43			8.026		9.208	9.505	114	113

Source: Sen, op. cit., Table 2.

Figure 7.1 Space for Diagram in Answer to Question 4

Figure 7.2 Space for Diagram in Answer to Question 7

Question 5 On your diagram, show the endowment point for each
family if:
  (a) one family produces only fish and the other rice
      (label this A);
  (b) both families produce equal amounts of fish and
      rice (label this B);
  (c) one family produces half the fish and all the rice
      (label this C).

Question 6 (a) For each of the endowment points you drew for
Question 5, show whether it will be advantageous for
the families to trade.
(b) Show the region(s) of mutual advantage and the
contract curve.
(c) What assumptions are you making about the nature
of the exchange process?
(d) If families have identical tastes, will they derive any
advantage from trading?

Question 7 (a) Now draw another Edgeworth–Bowley box (as
Figure 7.2), the same size as before, but this time draw
the indifference maps of the two families so that the
marginal rate of substitution for Family 2 is greater than
that of Family 1 (let Family 1's origin be in the bottom
left-hand corner of the box) at endowment point A.
(b) Is it possible for the contract curve to lie along one
side of the box?
Use page 65 for your diagram.

Question 8 Now consider Figure 7.3. The families' endowment
point is shown as point E.
(a) A price line is drawn through the endowment point
(line p). What is the market rate of exchange of fish for
rice (or rice for fish)?
(b) What quantities of fish and rice will each family
wish to have? Do these represent a feasible outcome?
(c) What would you expect to happen to the prices of
the two commodities?

Question 9 Figure 7.3 has been reproduced in Figure 7.4 but a new
price line has been drawn (p').
(a) Has the rate of exchange of fish for rice fallen or
risen?

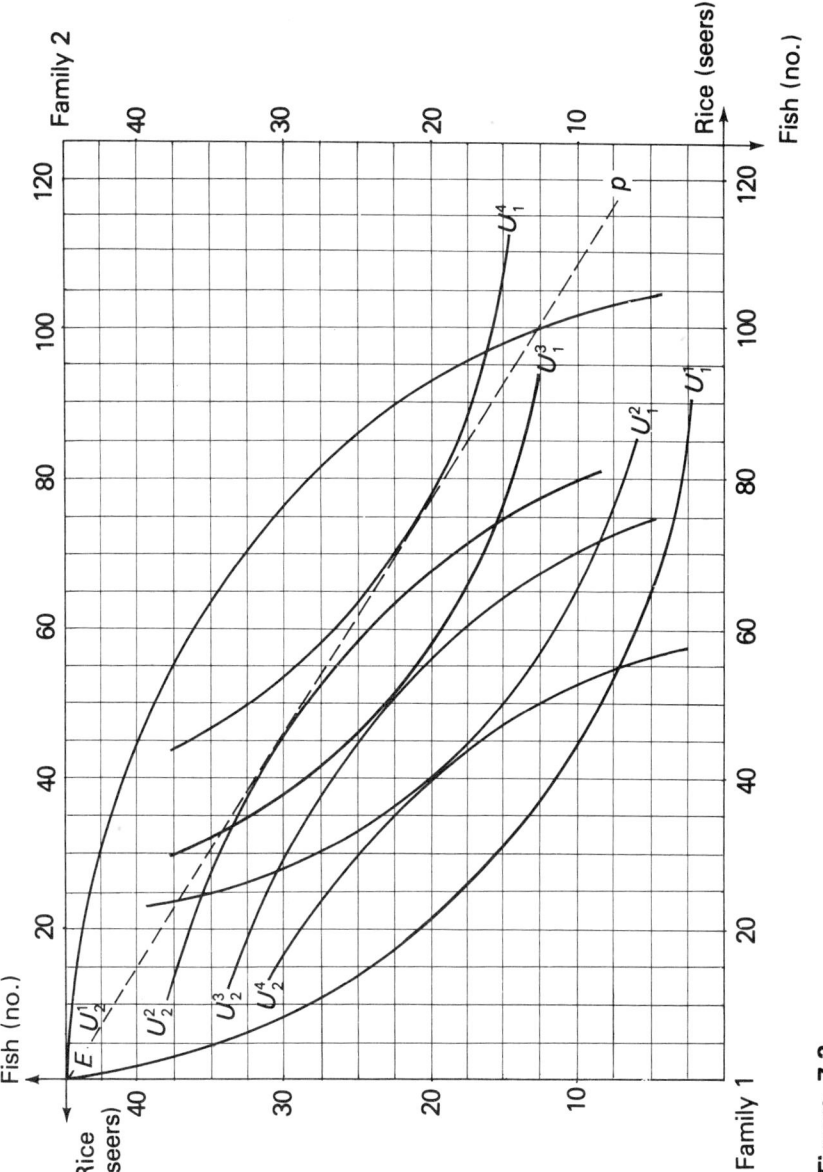

Figure 7.3

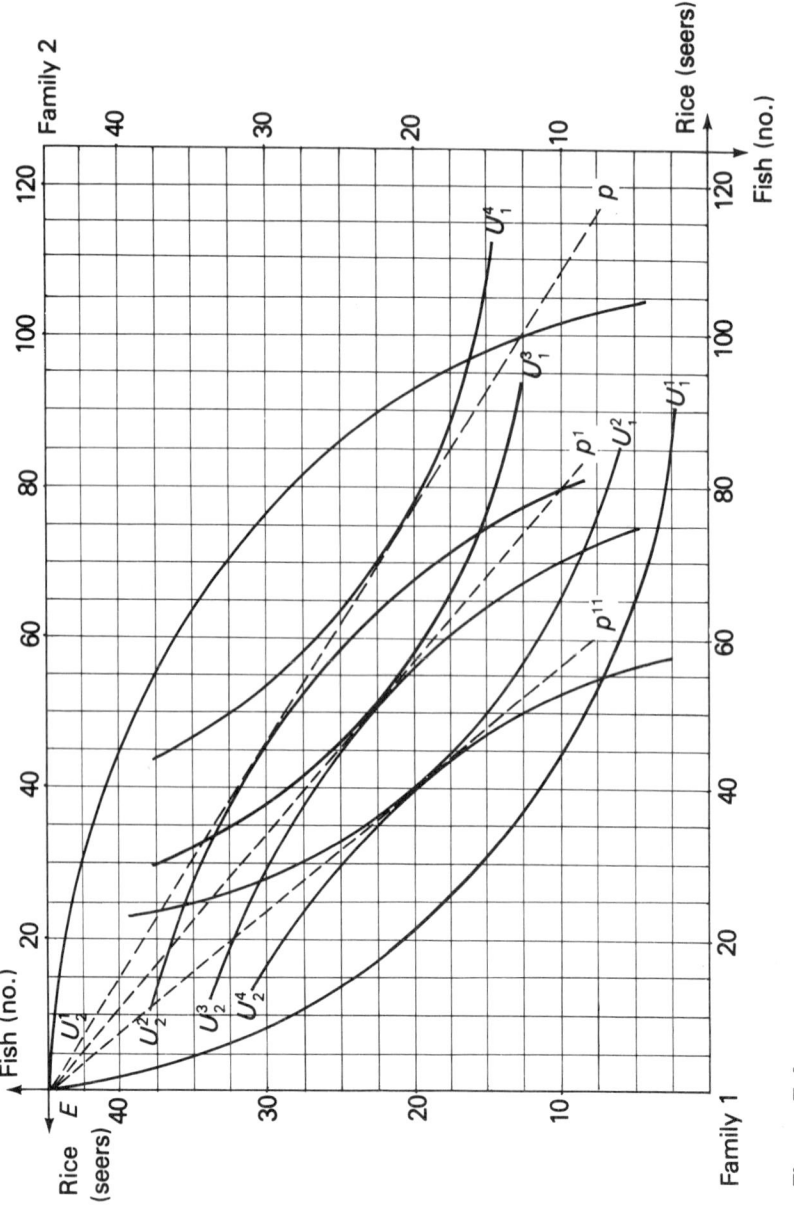

Figure 7.4

(b) Suppose that the price line were to change once more to p''. What is the exchange rate now? Explain in your own words which family is better off and why.

(c) Would it make any difference to your answers to (b) if both families produced something of each commodity instead of producing only fish or only rice?

Now we introduce an important new piece of information into the analysis. Suppose that indifference curve U_1^3 for Family 1 represents the survival set of combinations of fish and rice for that household, and that U_2^2 represents the survival set for Family 2. At prices p', both families survive although Family 1 is at subsistence level. However, when prices change to p'', the rate at which Family 1 can exchange fish for rice is insufficient to ensure its survival. It no longer makes sense to talk of 'preferences' and 'indifference curves' for bundles below those represented by indifference curves U_1^3 and U_2^2. What the analysis shows, however, is that when families are living at or near subsistence level, a rise in the price of the staple food may cause that family to starve — even if the price of what they have to offer in exchange also rises. As Sen says: '. . . whether a family will starve or not will depend on what it has to sell, whether it can sell them, and at what prices, and also on the price of food.' (op. cit., p. 34).

Question 10 Explain in your own words the meaning of 'exchange entitlements'.

Question 11 What data would you need to collect in order to test Sen's hypothesis that shifts in exchange entitlements brought rural families into destitution?

Question 12 Table 7.2 gives *imaginary* prices for rice and fish, and for daily wages. Calculate the price indices for rice, wages and fish, and then work out the relevant exchange rate, completing the table.

Question 13 As we mentioned, the data in Table 7.2 are imaginary but they have been chosen to show similar changes in the exchange rates as can be found in Tables 4 and 5 of Sen's article. When you have finished this exercise you can have a look at the real figures. In the meantime, if the figures in Table 7.2 were actual rather than imaginary figures, would they support Sen's thesis?

Table 7.2 Imaginary Daily Wages and Prices for Rice and Fish

Mid-month	Rice (Rs. per seer)	Rice price index	Wage (Rs. per day)	Wage index	Exchange rate index: labour vis-à-vis rice	Fish (Rs. per seer equivalent)	Fish price index	Exchange rate index: fish vis-à-vis rice
1941								
December	0.17	100	0.40	100	100	0.12	100	100
1942								
September	0.20	—	0.40	—	—	0.18	—	—
October	0.27	—	0.40	—	—	0.16	—	—
November	0.35	—	0.38	—	—	0.18	—	—
December	0.27	—	0.49	—	—	0.16	—	—
1943								
January	0.30	—	0.57	—	—	0.13	—	—
February	0.27	—	0.57	—	—	0.14	—	—
March	0.40	—	0.49	—	—	0.14	—	—
April	0.56	—	0.57	—	—	0.13	—	—
May	0.83	—	0.57	—	—	0.15	—	—
June	0.78	—	0.57	—	—	0.22	—	—
July	0.80	—	0.60	—	—	0.21	—	—
August	0.81	—	0.70	—	—	0.21	—	—
September	0.54	—	0.57	—	—	0.21	—	—
October	0.60	—	0.64	—	—	0.21	—	—
November	0.50	—	0.64	—	—	0.27	—	—
December	0.37	—	0.78	—	—	0.27	—	—
1944								
January	0.39	—	0.70	—	—	0.26	—	—

Question 14 (a) Why do you think the exchange rates rose in
December 1942 and December 1943?
(b) Were there any periods when the price of fish rose
but the exchange rate of fish vis-à-vis rice fell?

The more alert of you will be wondering why the price of rice rose in
Bengal if there was no acute shortage. This is discussed by Sen and if you are
interested you can follow this up in his article. Briefly, the reasons he suggests are demand shifts due to inflationary pressures from military and civil
construction for the war economy which was financed by printing notes,
and speculative buying and hoarding made worse by administrative
incompetence.

Question 15 Of the following occupational groups, which would be
most likely to suffer from the shift in exchange
entitlements and which would be the most protected?

(a) Peasant cultivation and share-cropping
(b) Agricultural labour
(c) Artisan
(d) Petty trader
(e) Cropsharing landlord
(f) Priest and petty employee
(g) Office employee
(h) Landlord

(When you read Sen's article, check your predictions
against his Table 8.)

Question 16 The important point Sen is making is that the
authorities, in attributing the cause of the famine to a
shortage of rice, were concentrating on one market —
the market for food grains — but the true explanation
was more complicated and required an understanding of
the interdependence of markets. It can be very
misleading to focus on one market and ignore the links
between markets, so be careful not to fall into the same
trap! If the authorities had understood the nature of the
problem, what action should they have taken?

Question 17 Has this problem any relevance for our economy? What
is your endowment, i.e. what have you to offer in
exchange for food and all the other things you want to
buy? What determines your endowment and the price
you obtain? If we all have only 24 hours a day, does

not everyone have an equal endowment? In this country, if there is an adverse shift in the terms of exchange,
what protects families from destitution? Can you give
examples of shifts in exchange entitlements for the UK?

Reference

*Sen, A.K. (1977) 'Starvation and exchange entitlements: a general approach and its
  application to the great Bengal famine', *Cambridge Journal of Economics*, 1,
  pp. 33–59.

---

* Suggested supplementary reading.

8

Economies of Scale in the Motor Industry

A monopolist can increase profits by price discrimination if it can divide its market. In this problem we ask what happens if demand falls off in one market: can the monopolist make up any losses by selling more in the remaining market(s)? The answer depends on the cost conditions the monopolist faces. We therefore start this problem by examining the factors that determine a firm's cost function in the short and long run. We explore the sources of economies of scale in the car industry in order to establish the minimum efficient scale of operation. This may be a term that you have not encountered before. The minimum efficient scale (MES) is that size of plant at which long-run average costs are at a minimum. This plant size may not be unique as empirical evidence suggests that many firms may face L-shaped long-run average cost curves. If demand for a firm's product is such that it cannot produce at the minimum efficient scale, then the price the firm charges is likely to be higher than that of any competitors producing at the MES. The level of production at which the MES is achieved is therefore important in determining the competitiveness of any industry.

Check your understanding of the following before working through the problem:

(a) *average and marginal revenue;*
(b) *price elasticity of demand;*
(c) *the law of diminishing returns;*
(d) *constant, increasing and decreasing returns to scale;*
(e) *the firm's least-cost condition;*
(f) *the firm's output expansion path;*
(g) *the conditions under which price discrimination is possible;*
(h) *the profit-maximising solution where market segmentation is possible.*

When analysing the performance of an industry, we need to consider whether firms are producing under conditions of economies or diseconomies of scale. To illustrate the importance of establishing the nature of cost conditions facing a firm we consider the British motor industry and, in particular, BL.

There is no need to remind you of BL's problems. We will not attempt here to analyse all the factors that have contributed to its difficulties; in this exercise we shall concentrate on the relationship between demand and supply conditions — in particular, on the shape of the long-run average cost curves — and examine the position of BL in the 1960s[1] when the UK motor industry was in a happier condition than it is now. At that time it produced nearly two million cars with production peaking in 1964. By the end of the 1960s about 45 per cent of production was exported and imports were approximately 10 per cent of new registrations (Pratten 1971, p. 132).

Question 1 Look at Table 8.1. How did BL's production compare with that of other manufacturers in 1966?

In the 1950s and 1960s, the economy was run on a 'stop-go' pattern (see Dow 1964 and Caves and Associates 1968). When the government wished to restrict domestic demand, a frequently used instrument was that of credit restriction, either by requiring larger deposits or by raising the interest rates for hire purchase (see Caves, op. cit., pp. 77—78). Whenever such restrictions were introduced, the motor industry was one of the first to suffer as demand for its products fell away. The government, however, was unsympathetic to the industry's protests and argued that producers could recoup any losses from falling home sales by increasing exports.

Was the government correct? This is the question taken up by Jennings (1970). He asks: do high levels of home sales go together with a successful export performance or does depressing home demand have a favourable effect on exports? Note that we are concerned with demand for cars in two markets — home and abroad. Jennings uses the model of a price discriminating monopolist to examine this question and his analysis highlights the importance of taking into account the nature of the cost curves faced by the firm. This problem is adapted from his article.

Question 2 What conditions are necessary for BL to be able to adopt a policy of price discrimination?

---

1. In the 1960s BL was known as the British Motor Corporation and since that time the company has undergone various changes, including a change of name. In order to avoid confusion, we shall refer to the company as BL throughout this exercise.

Table 8.1 Car Production by UK and Selected Foreign Manufacturers

Production	1966	1970	1975	1980	1983
UK					
BL*	788,194	788,737	605,141	395,820	473,341
% exported	40	47	43	40	30
Talbot/Dodge	171,904	216,995	226,612	125,314	120,503
% exported	29	46	71	75	70
Ford	466,177	448,422	329,648	342,767	318,674
% exported	41	41	27	25	10
Vauxhall	172,777	178,089	98,621	55,002	126,524
% exported	37	37	22	18	0.25
Other	4,627	8,723	7,673	4,841	5,555
% exported	53	38	52	44	32
UK total	1,603,679	1,640,966	1,267,695	923,744	1,044,597
% exported	39	44	42	38	23
France					
Renault	666,224	1,055,803	1,042,261	1,492,339	1,639,405
Other	1,119,682	1,402,235	1,503,893	1,446,242	1,321,418
Total	1,785,906	2,458,038	2,546,154	2,938,581	2,960,823
West Germany					
Opel	649,376	811,640	655,877	786,663	934,490
VW	1,392,491	1,518,365	1,050,286	1,232,164	1,097,834
Other	788,633	1,197,859	1,201,656	1,502,107	1,845,317
Total	2,830,500	3,527,864	2,907,819	3,520,934	3,877,641
Italy					
Fiat	—	1,514,376	1,078,007	1,072,040	1,157,830
Other	—	205,339	270,537	373,181	237,701
Total	1,282,418	1,719,715	1,348,544	1,445,221	1,395,531
Japan					
Honda	32,599	276,844	328,107	845,514	857,686
Nissan	253,046	899,008	1,532,731	1,940,615	1,858,782
Toyo	92,143	224,520	387,411	736,544	861,580
Toyota	316,189	1,068,321	1,714,836	2,303,284	2,380,753
Other	183,679	710,015	605,035	1,212,151	1,193,087
Total	877,656	3,178,708	4,568,120	7,038,108	7,151,888

Source: Society of Motor Manufacturers and Traders Ltd, *The Motor Industry of Great Britain*.
Note: * 1966, 1970, 1975 and 1980: Austin-Morris, Triumph, Rover, Jaguar-Daimler. 1983: Austin-Rover, Jaguar-Daimler, Range Rover.

Question 3 Do you think that the elasticity of demand for BL's cars
was the same in both markets? Draw appropriate
demand schedules (linear for simplicity) on Figure 8.1.

Question 4 What are the profit-maximising conditions?

Before we can find the profit-maximising output levels for the two
markets we need to draw in the relevant cost curves. We must therefore
establish whether BL was facing decreasing, constant or increasing costs, and
before we turn to the empirical evidence, we review the underlying theory.

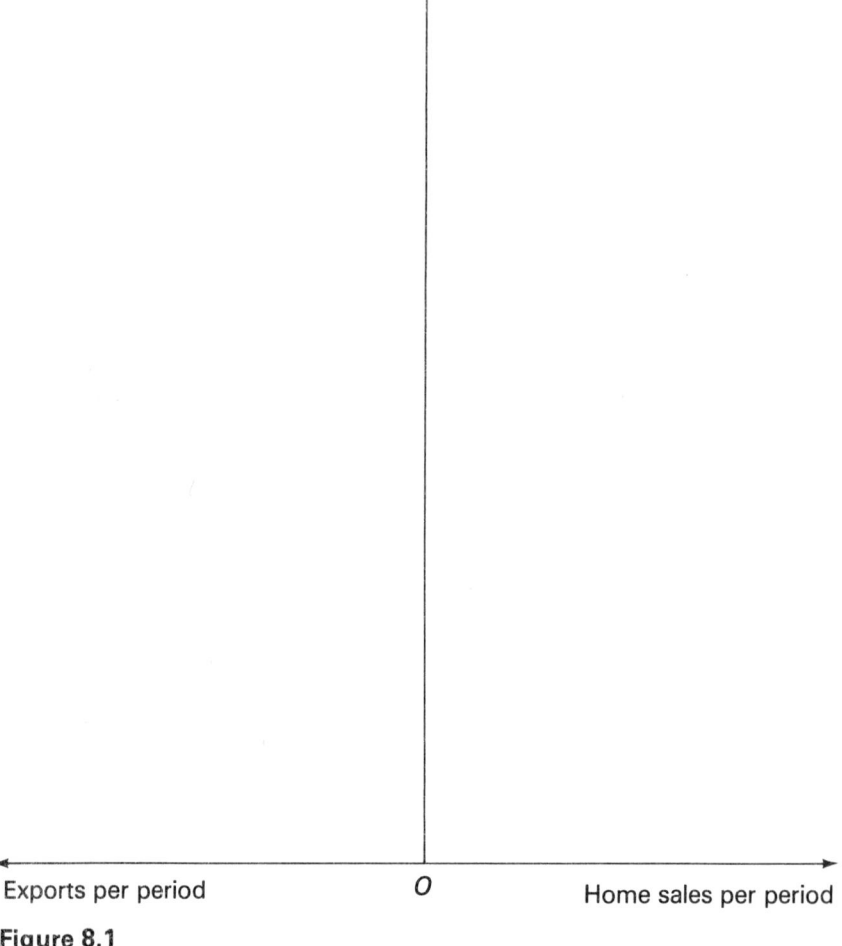

Figure 8.1

Question 5   What factors determine a firm's cost function?

$$C = c(\qquad)$$

Question 6   If a firm is facing decreasing costs, then it experiences economies of scale. Define 'economies of scale'.

Question 7   On Figure 8.2 show how a firm's expansion path is derived. If capital is fixed, show that higher output is achieved at a higher average cost than would be the case if both inputs were varied.

Figure 8.2

Question 8   Suppose that both factor prices increase by the same
proportion. What would happen to the expansion path?
What would be the effect on average cost?

Question 9   What happens to the expansion path if the price of one
input rises?

Question 10 If a firm experiences capital-deepening technological
progress, what happens to the marginal rate of technical
substitution?

Question 11 Various short-run total cost curves are shown in Figure
8.3. How do you find the long-run total cost curve?
What do the intercepts, T_1, T_2, etc., represent?

Question 12 On Figure 8.4 trace out short-run and long-run average
cost curves taking care to relate these curves to the total
cost curves drawn in Figure 8.3. Repeat for the marginal
cost curves.

Question 13 When is short-run marginal cost equal to long-run
marginal cost?

Question 14 What is meant by 'minimum efficient scale'? At what
output level is it reached in your diagram on Figure 8.4?

Question 15 Suppose that, for whatever reason, a firm's output is
half that necessary for production at the minimum efficient scale. Show on your diagram the effect on costs.

Question 16 What determines whether a firm will operate at its
minimum efficient scale?

Question 17 We now look at estimates of economies of scale in the
car industry but, before you read on, list possible
sources of production economies of scale.

Car production is a complicated operation involving different processes,
each of which gives rise to economies of scale. There are four main processes:
pressing; forge and foundry; engine and transmission; and final assembly. A
completely new model entails high initial costs in that new dies have to be
made for the body panels, new moulds for the engine, specialised machine
tools, etc. If it is possible to use the same engine in different models, and
some of the same panels, then production runs in the relevant processes will
be longer and change-over costs reduced. The first three processes all reap
considerable economies from automation; final assembly is more labour

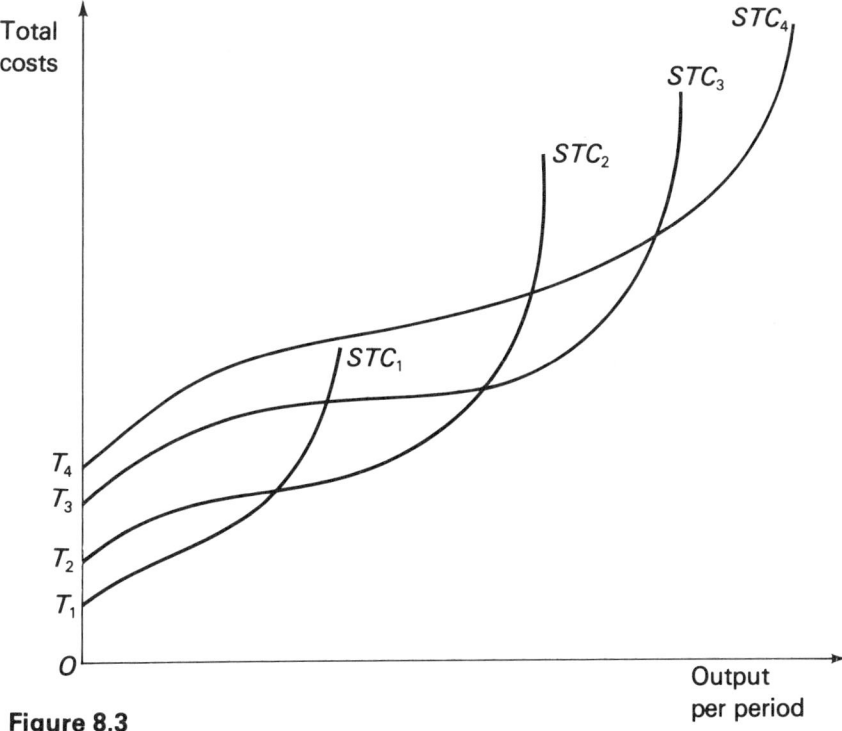

Figure 8.3

Figure 8.4

intensive but permits economies through specialisation on the assembly line. (For more information see Pratten (1971), McGee (1973) on pressing, and Owen (1983).)

Table 8.2 gives various estimates of minimum efficient scales for the different processes. Changes in technology over the last ten years have raised minimum scales and Owen suggests that the optimal level of production is currently around two million cars per annum (1983, p. 75).

Table 8.2 Estimates of Minimum Efficient Scales

Output (thousands p.a.)	Pressing	Forge and foundry	Engine and transmission	Final assembly
Pratten[1]	500	1000	250	300
Rhys[2]	2000	200	1000	200
Bhaskar[3]	500+	1000—2000	400—1000	200—400

Notes: (1) Pratten (1971), p. 128 and pp. 136—141
       (2) Rhys (1972), p. 289.
       (3) Bhaskar (1979), p. 25.

Question 18 If a car manufacturer could produce at minimum efficient scale, how many plants would he need for each process given the following estimates?

	Pressing	Forge and foundry	Engine and transmission	Final assembly
Output (thousands per annum)	2000	2000	1000	250

As no EC manufacturers approach an output of two million cars per annum, it is of great interest to estimate the amount by which costs rise as output falls below the minimum efficient scale. Owen's estimate is that unit costs fall by about ten per cent each time output is doubled (op. cit., p. 75).

At last we can find an answer to the question of whether a decline in home demand can be offset by higher export sales. Draw in appropriate long-run average and marginal cost curves for BL on Figure 8.1 and find the profit-maximising output and price for both markets.

Question 19 Does BL charge the same price for home and export sales?

Question 20 Now suppose that as a result of credit restrictions, demand falls in the home market. What happens to sales in the home and export markets? Will prices change? What happens to total sales?

Question 21 Owen's estimates indicate that BL is currently producing at less than minimum efficient scale. The minimum efficient scale for a firm will vary industry by industry. In order to round off your analysis, check out whether a price-discriminating monopolist's total sales rise or fall when average costs are constant or rising. In other words, does the conclusion you reached as to whether exports can offset a fall in home sales depend on the nature of the cost curve facing the monpolist? Redraw Figure 8.1 and analyse the two other possibilities. Summarize your results in Table 8.3.

Table 8.3

	Decreasing costs	Constant costs	Increasing costs
Export market ⎰ sales	_____	_____	_____
⎱ price	_____	_____	_____
Home market ⎰ sales	_____	_____	_____
⎱ price	_____	_____	_____
Total sales	_____	_____	_____

Owen's estimates of minimum efficient scale and associated cost penalties in the car industry form part of a larger study of trade within the European Community where his major focus is on the role of economies of scale. The chapter on the European car industry provides an excellent example of the importance of market size and of scale economies, and you may also be interested in his comparison of BL's unit costs with those of its competitors in the Community (1983, Ch. 4).

Have British car manufacturers practised price discrimination? Ashworth, Kay and Sharp of the Institute for Fiscal Studies concluded that, on average, discounted prices net of tax were 38.5 per cent higher in the UK than in Belgium (1982, p. 9). Explanations, other than price discrimination, which they considered were: restrictions on Japanese imports; slow price adaptation to changing market circumstances; and collusion amongst distributors or manufacturers. Voluntary restriction meant that Japanese sales were only

11 per cent of total UK sales at the time of their study. As can be inferred from Table 8.1, some Japanese firms must be low cost producers compared with British firms and, with restrictions on imports, the Japanese might have been expected to raise prices to eliminate any excess demand. However, the Institute for Fiscal Studies' report found the Japanese differential to be 25 per cent, i.e. less than the average, suggesting that the whole explanation is not to be found here. Similarly, sluggish price changes — for example, in response to changes in the real exchange rate — may explain part but not all of the difference. The authors of the report found no evidence of collusion and thus turned to consider what might cause differences in demand for British cars in home and foreign markets. If foreign cars are not considered to be close substitutes for British cars in the British market, this would enable British manufacturers to set higher prices, especially if they held the major market share. The elasticity of substitution of foreign for British-made cars may be low because the British, like other nationalities, exhibit national preferences for national products. This may be for patriotic reasons but domestic products are generally backed up by strong distribution networks for sales and spare parts. Moreover, one would expect manufacturers to design cars to reflect the taste of domestic consumers. British companies prefer to 'Buy British' when providing cars for their managers, and sales to companies form a large proportion of total domestic sales (see Ashworth, Kay and Sharp, op. cit., Table 12).

Question 22 Did you think of these points when answering Question 3?

Question 23 If British companies are to operate successful price discrimination, they must be able to separate the markets. When it became known that it was possible to buy British cars cheaper in Europe, newspapers carried reports of purchasers making trips across the Channel to buy their new cars. At the price differential, the trip was well worthwhile. How might British manufacturers attempt to prevent such purchases? Did you cover this point when you answered Question 2?

References

Ashworth, M.H., Kay, J.A. and Sharpe, T.A.E. (1982) *Differentials between Car Prices in the United Kingdom and Belgium*, Institute for Fiscal Studies Report, Series No. 2.
Bhaskar, Krish (1979) *The Future of the UK Motor Industry*, Kogan Page.
Caves, R.E. and Associates (1968) *British Economic Prospects*, Brooking and George Allen and Unwin.

Dow, J.C.R. (1964) *The Management of the British Economy, 1945—60*, National Institute of Economic and Social Research, Cambridge University Press.

*Jennings, A. (1970) 'Government policy and the British motor industry's export performance', *Applied Economics*, 2, pp. 65—72.

McGee, John S. (1973) 'Economies of size in auto-body manufacture', *Journal of Law and Economics*, 16, pp. 239—273.

*Owen, Nicholas (1983) *Economies of Scale, Competitiveness, and Trade Patterns within the European Community*, Oxford University Press.

*Pratten, C.F. (1971) *Economies of Scale in Manufacturing Industry*, Cambridge University Press.

Rhys, D.G. (1972) *The Motor Industry: An Economic Survey*, Butterworths.

Central Policy Review Staff (1975) *The Future of the British Car Industry*, HMSO.

---

* Suggested supplementary reading.

9

Regulation of Taxis

The usual textbook model of a monopoly is an industry consisting of one firm. There are, however, few natural monopolies and sometimes it is the government which sets up a barrier, thus restricting entry to a market and creating a monopoly. In such cases, the government generally regulates the activities of the successful entrants. One example of such a monopoly is to be found in the taxi services of many towns and cities. In this problem we ask you to consider whether it is to the advantage of the consumer that restrictions are placed on entry into the taxicab business. One result of limiting entry is that the fare charged is likely to be higher than would be the case if the market were competitive. We consider how we can make a monetary estimate of any welfare loss arising from higher prices and make use of information about the taxi markets in Birmingham and Manchester.

Before starting work on the problem, check your understanding of the following:

(a) types of barriers to entry to markets;
(b) demand and supply in competitive and monopoly markets;
(c) monopoly and economic efficiency;
(d) consumer and producer surplus;
(e) welfare loss of monopoly;
(f) economic rent;
(g) alternative ways of regulating a monopoly.

Taxis are one of several forms of transport available in most towns and cities but whereas buses or the railways may be state owned, taxis are privately owned. In general, taxi services are regulated by local authorities, but the form of regulation may differ between areas. In London, persons whose taxis conform to the permitted specification (for example, taxis must meet certain safety requirements) and who can display the required extensive knowledge of routes and locations, may obtain a licence to 'ply for hire'. This means that taxis can be hired on the streets, either while cruising or when at ranks, unlike private hire cars which must be pre-booked by the customer, usually by telephone.

In many other areas, including Birmingham, the situation is rather different. Would-be taxi owner-drivers have to show the required knowledge and their vehicles have to satisfy official standards, as in London, but only a *limited* number of licence plates are issued by the licensing authority.[1] This means that at any time there may be a waiting list for licence plates and any taxi owner retiring from the taxi business can sell his plate to the highest bidder. Prices vary but may be substantial and can exceed £10,000 (see Coe and Jackson, op. cit.; also Price Commission 1978).

On 30 July 1980 *The Birmingham Post* carried a report that Birmingham taxi drivers were planning to stage a mass demonstration for about an hour on 31 July; further demonstrations were planned for every Tuesday and Thursday up to 19 August. The taxi drivers were protesting about Birmingham City Council's plan to issue new licences. The following is an extract from *The Birmingham Post*'s report:

> The controversial licence decision was taken by the City General Purposes Committee last week to reduce the waiting list of 432. The Birmingham Licensed Taxi Owners' and Drivers' Association claimed there was not enough work for the 430 taxis already operating.
>
> The taxi drivers have been warned by the Association that anyone accepting the new licences will be considered not to be acting in the best interests of the trade. As a result they could be denied radio facilities and access to Birmingham Airport, the National Exhibition Centre and New Street Station.
>
> Not all taxi drivers are behind the Association; several have contacted the City Council. One claims that the taxi drivers' leaders are multi-owners, who could lose drivers with more licences issued, and more licences would reduce the going rate for a licence of between £5000 and £6000.

Question 1 Can you think of any reasons why local authorities should regulate entry into the taxi market?

Question 2 Can you suggest why they might choose to restrict the *number* of licence plates they issue, regardless of the number of suitably qualified applicants?

---

1. Approximately 80 per cent of licensing authorities in England and Wales restrict the number of taxi licence plates, but the degree of restriction varies from authority to authority. For example, in Liverpool the number of licence plates issued results in one taxi per 472 persons whereas in Manchester there is one taxi per 1053 persons (Coe and Jackson 1983).

Question 3 Private hire cars do not have to be licensed, although about sixty per cent of licensing authorities do operate a licensing system. However, the number of licences may not be restricted. Can you suggest any reason why private hire cars should be treated differently from taxis?

Question 4 What do you think determines the price of taxi licence plates? If no new plates had been issued in Birmingham since 1980, do you think that the price of a plate would be the same today as it was when the taxi drivers were protesting? Is the demand for taxi plates a derived demand?

Question 5 If the only form of regulation of the taxi market were the form of licensing adopted by London (i.e. no restriction on numbers), would you expect taxi fares in Birmingham to be the same as in London? (In fact fares are regulated in both these cities, but ignore this for the moment.)

Question 6 If fares were determined by market forces, when comparing taxi fares in the two cities we need to consider both the demand and the supply conditions. Is it likely that the demand for taxis is similar in Birmingham and London? What about London and your home town?

Question 7 How close a substitute are private hire cars for taxis? Does it make any difference whether you are considering short or long trips?

Question 8 Having briefly considered the demand for taxis, we return to the supply side. In both cities regulation imposes entry costs. List the categories of costs faced by a successful entrant in London and in Birmingham. Will a taxi owner in Birmingham face higher or lower initial costs than one in London?

Question 9 The taxi drivers' protest in Birmingham did not succeed in preventing the issue of new licences: in August 1980 the Council started to issue new plates to people on the waiting list. No-one who already held a licence plate could obtain another. In your opinion, how fair was it to existing taxi owners that the Council issued additional plates?

Question 10 In May 1982 Birmingham City Council (now Conser-
vative) suspended the issue of new licence plates and
closed the waiting list — the current number of plates in
Birmingham is 549. As no new plates are being issued,
anyone wishing to enter the taxi business in Birmingham as a taxi owner has, once again, to purchase a
plate from a retiring driver. By January 1985 the price
of such a plate had fallen and was possibly not more
than £500. Have all taxi owners experienced losses as a
result of the Council issuing additional licences?

The fall in price cannot be fully explained by the increase in the number of
plates; the current high unemployment rate in Birmingham, together with
discounting against the possibility that the Council might once again issue
plates at some future time, would also cause the value to drop. Did you think
of these points when answering Question 4?

We now consider the costs and benefits of taxi regulation. When entry
numbers are restricted by limiting the issue of licence plates, taxi users
experience a loss of welfare for two main reasons. Firstly, the premium that
taxi owners have to pay to acquire a licence plate is passed on to the users in
the form of higher fares. Secondly, if there are fewer taxis plying for hire,
then customers may have less chance of quickly picking up a passing taxi
when they want it, or may have to wait longer for one at the taxi rank.

We start by attempting to measure the welfare loss arising from the
increase in fares. We can measure this loss by estimating the change in consumer surplus and finding the 'deadweight loss' (see Harberger 1954).

Question 11 Define consumer surplus.

Question 12 Figure 9.1 shows a demand curve for taxi trips. What is
the change in consumer surplus when fares rise from P_1
to P_2? How much of the loss to consumers represents a
transfer of income from consumers to producers and
how much is the 'deadweight loss'?

Question 13 What information do we need in order to measure the
deadweight loss?

We start by assuming that the average number of trips made by a taxi in a
year amounts to 8,650. This figure is taken from Beesley (1973) who made an
estimate of the welfare loss from regulating taxis in Birmingham in the early
1970s. At the time he was writing, he considered the average fare to be 30p;
allowing for inflation, we assume that the average fare had risen to £1.50 by

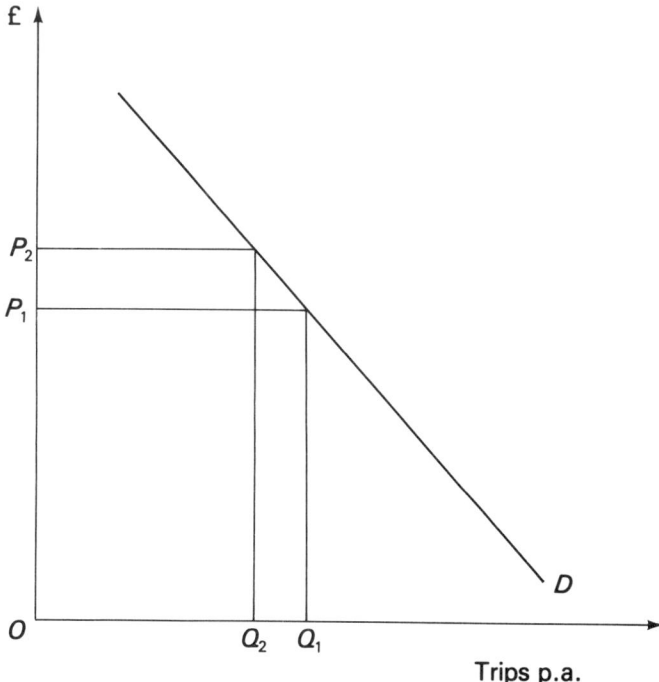

Figure 9.1

1980. Now, any would-be entrant to the taxi market in Birmingham at that time had to pay £5,000 or more for a plate (see extract from *The Birmingham Post* quoted earlier). He could enter the private hire car market without paying any premium, as you will remember there are no restrictions on entry there. The price of the licence plate approximates the discounted value of the flow of net expected earnings. Clearly any purchaser must take into account the possibility that such earnings may not continue forever and he must also consider what alternative rate of return he could get on the £5,000 he has to pay for the plate. Let us assume that the discount rate is 15 per cent; any purchaser then expects to get a net return of at least £750 p.a. and this, spread over 8,650 trips per annum, suggests that fares would be approximately 9p lower if no premium were payable for licence plates. Given that the average fare was £1.50 in 1980, this means that if entry had been unrestricted, the average fare would have been £1.41.[2] We now have to make some assump-

---

2. As we have already mentioned, taxi fares are regulated. We assume here that the average fare for unrestricted entry covers costs and allows for normal profits.

tion about the elasticity of demand in order to estimate the change in the number of trips. Allen took this to be 'around or rather below unity' in 1953 (*Runciman Committee on the Taxicab Service*, 1953, Appendix V, para. 5).

Question 14 An elasticity of unity seems likely to be rather low for 1985 (why?); nevertheless, take this value and work out the change in trips generated by a price fall of 9p.

Question 15 The annual deadweight loss for each cab equals:

½ (change in trips) (change in price)

assuming a linear demand curve. Work out this welfare loss.

Question 16 You can now fill in figures for P_1, P_2, Q_1 and Q_2 on Figure 9.1. You may be interested to learn that Beesley estimated this loss to be £17.50 per annum per cab in the early 1970s (Beesley, op. cit., p. 159).

Question 17 You may think that a discount rate of 15 per cent was too high or too low. If you think a higher rate would be more appropriate, would this raise or lower your estimate of the welfare loss, *ceteris paribus*?

Question 18 What if the elasticity of demand were greater than unity? Would this mean the welfare loss was larger or smaller?

Question 19 As we noted earlier, the price of a licence plate in Birmingham has fallen greatly since 1980. If it is currently £500, would this mean that current taxi users experience a significant welfare loss?

Before you continue with the rest of the problem you might like to make quite sure you have understood how the deadweight loss is calculated. If you wish, you can repeat the exercise by measuring such a loss for Manchester in 1982 using the information given in the Appendix at the end of this problem.

You will remember that we also mentioned that users could experience a welfare loss if the quality of the taxi service were lower when entry is restricted. One aspect of quality is the ready availability of taxis.

Question 20 Can you think of any other dimensions of quality for a taxi service?

Beesley has attempted to measure the welfare loss arising from lower availability of taxis in his article (op. cit.) and we shall not attempt a measure here. However, there are some problems that arise in deriving an estimate of this type of welfare loss.

Question 21 Before reading on, think whether you would be prepared to pay more in order to be sure of picking up a taxi within a short period of time.
(a) What do you think is a reasonable waiting period?
(b) If you would be prepared to pay more, how much more would you be willing to pay? Would the amount depend on the time of day?

The availability of a taxi depends on not only the number of taxis plying for hire in any district but also the number of hours per day that each taxi is operated. There are currently 900 licensed drivers in Birmingham, not all of whom may be active, and 549 taxis. Taxis can be double-shifted, that is to say the taxi owner drives it for one shift and sub-contracts it for another (or alternatively employs a driver). The Price Commission reported that, on average, owner-drivers worked 50 hours per week, sub-contractors 53 and employees 48 (Price Commission 1978, Table 4.5). If, in areas where there is restriction on the number of taxis, the vehicles are more intensively used than in those where there is no restricted entry, then it could be that both areas end up with a similar number of hours of taxi services being provided in any given time period. One way to measure the availability of the service is to monitor the waiting time of passengers and see if they have to wait longer periods when entry numbers are restricted. Similarly, if we find that taxi waiting times are longer in unrestricted areas, it seems likely that taxis will be more readily available. Unfortunately there is no published information on average waiting times for taxis and passengers in Birmingham. The Price Commission, however, has provided such information for Liverpool and Manchester in 1978. These two cities have roughly the same population but entry is more liberal in Liverpool (842 taxis in 1978) than in Manchester (408 in 1978) (Price Commission, op. cit., Table 4.2). The Commission's survey shows that waiting times (in minutes) for the hours between eight in the morning and six at night varied from 0.2 to 2.6 for passengers waiting at Manchester Piccadilly Station and from no waiting to 0.6 in Manchester's Albert Square. In Liverpool, passenger waiting times varied from zero to 1.1 minutes at Lime Street Station and from zero to 0.2 in Church Street (Price Commission, op. cit., Tables 2 and 3, Appendix 4).

Question 22 In the light of your answers to Question 21, would you consider the quality of service in Manchester to be lower than you desire?

In Question 7 you were asked whether you considered private hire cars to be close substitutes for taxis. Coe and Jackson undertook a study of the effects of restrictions of taxi numbers and one of their findings was that, on average, taxis comprised 73 per cent of the combined taxi and private hire car fleets in areas where issue of plates was relatively generous, as against 29 per cent in areas where it was more tight (1983, p. 10). Their study was based on pairwise comparison of areas of high and low levels of taxi provision and six areas were matched with another six areas, as similar in character as possible with regard to population, geographical location, nature of main bus operator and socio-economic characteristics.

Question 23 Would greater availability of private hire cars in areas where taxi numbers were tightly controlled offset any possible loss of quality?

So far we have discussed the deadweight loss arising from restriction but have ignored any income transfers.

Question 24 What is the economic rent that a taxi owner receives following the purchase of a licence plate? What area of Figure 9.1 represents this rent?

Tullock (1967) and Posner (1975) have pointed out that the creation or acquisition of a monopoly, and its maintenance, involve the use of resources, and such resources represent a loss to society in general which should be included in any measure of the consequent welfare loss. Posner suggests:

> there is no reason to think that monopoly has a significant distributive effect. Consumers' wealth is not transferred to the shareholders of monopoly firms; it is dissipated in the purchase of inputs into the activity of becoming a monopolist. (op. cit., p. 821)

Question 25 What is the cost of obtaining a share in a monopoly in the taxi market?

Question 26 Will competition amongst would-be entrants affect this cost?

Question 27 Could the price of a licence plate reach a level such that it absorbs all the economic rent a taxi owner receives from his share in the monopoly?

Hillman and Katz argue that where a monopoly yields relatively small rents and monopoly-seekers are risk averse, then we can approximate the value of resources spent in obtaining the monopoly by taking the value of the economic rents it yields (1984, p. 107; see also Bhagwati 1982).

Question 28 Do you think this is the result found in the taxi market?

Question 29 Are there likely to be significant costs in maintaining the monopoly in a taxi market? If so, will these be reflected in the price paid for licence plates?

Question 30 Can you now estimate the additional monopoly cost for taxis in Birmirfgham in 1980 (and Manchester in 1982)?

We have concentrated on analysing the implications of restricting the number of licence plates. However, as we noted in the introduction, even if the number of plates were not restricted, would-be taxi owners and drivers may only enter the market if safety and route knowledge requirements are satisfied. In other words, there is still licensing but, in this form of licensing, all suitably qualified applicants can obtain plates. In Birmingham such licences currently cost £57 p.a. for a vehicle and £12 p.a. for each driver and are set to cover the administration costs. Once again, these costs are passed on in the form of higher fares to passengers and the corresponding welfare loss can be estimated.

Question 31 Are there any benefits to set against such licensing costs? Are you in favour of regulation of this type or do you think that entry should be completely free?

Price Regulation

From our analysis in the preceding section we would expect fares to be higher in markets where the number of entrants is restricted. We have mentioned earlier the study by Coe and Jackson in which they made pairwise comparisons of areas with high and low levels of taxi provision. They compared the fare levels and concluded that the differences between the two samples were not statistically significant (op. cit., p. 9). The fares in taxi markets are usually regulated by most licensing authorities. The regulated fare is a maximum fare and it would be possible for taxis to charge less than the official maximum; in practice, however, it is extremely unlikely that taxi drivers could compete in this way given that they pick up their customers while cruising or at ranks.

Question 32 Can you explain why their method of plying for hire
means that taxis are unlikely to charge less than the
official rate?

While this may explain why fares are unlikely to be forced down in the
competitive markets, it does not explain why we may observe a higher
regulated fare in the more open markets. A possible explanation might be
found in considering the difficulties authorities face in determining an
appropriate level of fare to set, given demand and supply conditions in their
area.

Question 33 Compare markets where (i) entry is restricted; (ii) entry
is open. At what level should the fare be set, bearing in
mind that this will determine not only the number of
trips but also the quality of the service (in terms of taxi
availability)? If there is pressure from the taxi owners
and drivers to raise the fare, under what circumstances
should price increases be agreed? Consider two
possibilities: (a) demand is inelastic; and (b) demand is
elastic.

Question 34 Private hire car fares are not regulated. Do you think
that taxi fares should be? In considering your answer
you might like to read the following extracts from a
letter to *The Times*, 27 August 1984:

> *Sir*: It seems to me to be self-evident that where govern-
> ment imposes prices below the market level there will be
> an unsatisfied demand for cab rides. When those con-
> trols are removed it is natural that prices will rise. ...
> Equilibrium will soon be restored at a price where an
> adequate demand by willing customers meets an ade-
> quate supply from willing sellers. Freedom for drivers to
> fix fares also eliminates the odious practice of tipping.
> (You) may not be aware that willing buyers at higher
> levels than the metered fare have established their own
> code of signals to attract drivers at times of scarcity of
> cabs. At 1 am on New Year's Day the pavement of the
> Haymarket is littered with gentlemen waving £5 or £10
> notes at passing cabs. ...
> Such practices could all be eliminated by allowing cab
> drivers to fix their own fares, which would be displayed
> as a rate per mile illuminated on the outside and inside
> of the cab. By arranging that the fare scale could not be
> changed once the meter was set, manipulation of the
> fare could be avoided.

After all, Sir, every coffee shop in London fixes its own price for a cup of coffee. It is not apparent that the general public is held to ransom. No one has to buy coffee, or take a cab ride. There is usually an alternative.

Cab drivers with the ability to fix their own fares will quickly find the level that keeps them working rather than waiting, to the benefit of both themselves and their customers.

Yours faithfully,
S.W. Pearce
(Licensed London cab driver no. 2239)

Question 35 This exercise has focused on regulation in one particular market. Before you finish, give some thought to the following questions:

(a) Are there other industries and/or professions where entry is restricted by licensing? Are licences issued to all suitably qualified applicants? Who determines whether the applicants are suitably qualified? Who does the licensing — is it always the government (central or local)?

(b) What other forms can regulation take?

References

*Beesley, M.E. (1973) 'Regulation of taxis', *Economic Journal*, 83, pp. 150–172.
Bhagwati, J.M. (1982) 'Directly unproductive, profit-seeking (DUP) activities', *Journal of Political Economy*, 90, pp. 988–1002.
Coe, G.A. and Jackson, R.L. (1983) *Some New Evidence Relating to Quality Control in the Taxi Industry*, Department of the Environment, Department of Transport, TRRL Supplementary Report 797, Transport and Road Research Laboratory.
*Harberger, Arnold C. (1954) 'Monopoly and resource allocation', *American Economic Review*, 44, May, pp. 277–288.
Hillman, A.L. and Katz, E. (1984) Risk-averse rent seekers and the social cost of monopoly power, *Economic Journal*, 94, pp. 104–110.
*Posner, Richard A. (1975) 'The social costs of monopoly and regulation', *Journal of Political Economy*, 83, pp. 807–827.
Tullock, Gordon (1967) 'The welfare costs of tariffs, monopolies, and theft', *Western Economic Journal*, 5, pp. 224–232.

Price Commission (1978) *Prices, Costs and Margins in the Provision of Taxicab and Private Hire Services*, HCC 655, HMSO.
Runciman Committee on the Taxicab Service (1953), Cmd. 8804, HMSO.

---

* Suggested supplementary reading.

Appendix

In 1982 there were 450 taxis in Manchester (representing an increase of ten per cent on 1978) and a licence plate cost between £11,000 and £12,000 (Coe and Jackson, op. cit., Price Commission, op. cit.).

The ratio of licensed drivers to taxis was 3:1 (Coe and Jackson) and it seems safe to assume that taxis would be used for double shifts. Using Price Commission figures on average hours worked per week, we estimate that a taxi would ply for hire 100 hours per week. In this way we arrive at a figure of 5,200 hours p.a. per cab.

The Price Commission found that the average number of trips per hour per cab was 2.1. However, this figure reflects a time when there were ten per cent fewer taxis. We therefore take the average trips per hour as 1.9 which means that, on average, a cab will undertake 9,880 trips p.a. in Manchester.

In 1978 the Price Commission estimated the average fare to be £1.07 for an average trip length of 3.3 miles. Coe and Jackson give fares for Manchester in 1982 of £1.35 (two people, two miles) and £2.45 (two people, four miles). Taking a slightly shorter trip length (to allow for the increase in taxis since 1978), a fare of £1.80 would not seem unreasonable.

10

OPEC – The Conservationists' Friend? Part I

The next two problems focus on the oil market. We start by analysing the factors that determine the price path of oil over time. As oil is a non-renewable resource, it is necessary to extend our understanding of the cost function of an oil producer. The costs of producing oil are not just the extraction costs: any producer has to bear in mind that if he sells a barrel of oil today, he has less oil to sell in the future. When equating marginal renevue and marginal cost, he must make sure that his estimate of marginal cost takes account of the opportunity cost of selling the oil today in order to make sure that he does not deplete his stock of oil too rapidly. We shall see that because oil is a non-renewable resource, its price will rise over time but the rate at which it rises depends on whether the market is perfectly or imperfectly competitive. The first part of the problem therefore considers the demand and supply factors that will influence the price of oil and provides the basis for analysing the role of OPEC in the oil market which is the subject of Problem 11.

The model we use in Problem 10 will be new to you as very few textbooks cover this topic. However, with the exception of marginal user cost, *which is explained on page 98, the theory we use can be found in any standard textbook. As long as you understand the meaning of marginal cost, are aware how demand curves are derived, understand discounting, and know the profit-maximising conditions for a competitive firm and for a monopolist, you should not find any new terms. The only unfamiliar part of the problem is the two-period model we use. It may take a little while to grasp the ideas it contains, but once you have managed this the rest of the exercise will be straightforward.*

Scarcely a month goes by without some reference to OPEC in the newspapers. Its regular meetings are reported with much speculation about the conflict of interests over its pricing and output decisions, and OPEC's collapse has been forecast at intervals since it was set up in 1960. In the second part of this exercise we shall examine the forces that lead oil producers to collaborate and those that threaten such co-operation. However, before we can do this we must spend a little time studying the production and pricing decisions of any owner of an exhaustible resource.

The firm usually studied in textbooks sells some commodity which it produces with renewable resources. The firm purchases inputs such as labour, capital and raw materials and its production costs are thus determined by the prices it pays for these and the technology it adopts. An oil producer also requires labour and capital. However, these are not used to make the product — oil — but to extract it from the earth. Oil is a primary product and the oil producer knows that if he extracts a barrel of oil today, he will have one less barrel to extract tomorrow. There is a finite stock of oil and as he draws off the oil over time, there will come a day when the oil well will run dry. In short, oil is an exhaustible resource.

Question 1 Can you think of other exhaustible resources? Is land an exhaustible resource?

Question 2 What are the main purposes for which oil is used?

Question 3 Does oil have characteristics which affect its demand and supply and make it different from other exhaustible resources such as iron ore?

The owner of an oil well has a valuable asset but in order to maximise its value he must exercise care in deciding at what rate to extract the oil. The more he sells this year, the less he will have to sell in future years. Assuming that he wishes to maximise long-run profits, he will wish to set marginal revenue equal to marginal cost, but what is the marginal cost of a barrel of oil? If we ignore transportation costs, then the cost consists of extraction costs and also the net revenue he foregoes by selling the oil today rather than in some future period. This foregone revenue is the opportunity or user cost. The marginal cost of a barrel of oil in any period is thus the sum of the marginal extraction cost (MEC) and the marginal user cost (MUC).

Question 4 The marginal user cost in any period is the net revenue for that period, i.e. $MUC_t = MR_t - MEC_t$. If the market for oil were perfectly competitive, what is the marginal user cost?

$$MUC_t =$$

Question 5 The firm's decision to sell oil in the current period or in future periods depends on how current prices compare with expected future prices. If the net price of a barrel of oil is $20 in the current period and you expect it to be $24 next year, would you hold back current production in order to sell more next year? (Assume that you can vary production costlessly.) What factors influence your decision?

In order to maximise long-run profits, an oil producer should sell his oil so that

$$MUC_0 = \frac{MUC_1}{(1+r)} = \frac{MUC_2}{(1+r)^2} = \cdots = \frac{MUC_T}{(1+r)^T}$$

where r is the discount rate. What this means is that a producer should deplete his well at a rate which leaves him indifferent between producing one extra barrel now and in any future period.

Question 6 Suppose that extraction costs are zero.[1] Suppose also that the market for oil is perfectly competitive. How would you write the condition for maximising profits in the long run?

Question 7 By what amount will prices change from period to period?

In order to examine the production flow in a perfectly competitive market, we simplify the problem and assume that there are only two periods. At the end of the second period oil stocks are exhausted. We also assume that the demand curves for oil are known for both periods, that the stock of oil is known and that extraction costs are zero. All these assumptions will be relaxed later.

In Figure 10.1 the market demand curves are shown for the two periods and the stock of oil is OS.

Question 8 Why is the demand curve for Period 2 shown as sloping downwards from right to left? How do we show oil sales in Period 2?

---

1. This is not so unrealistic as you might think. Extraction costs are very low in the Middle East fields: Danielsen states that they are less than a dollar a barrel (1982, p. 29).

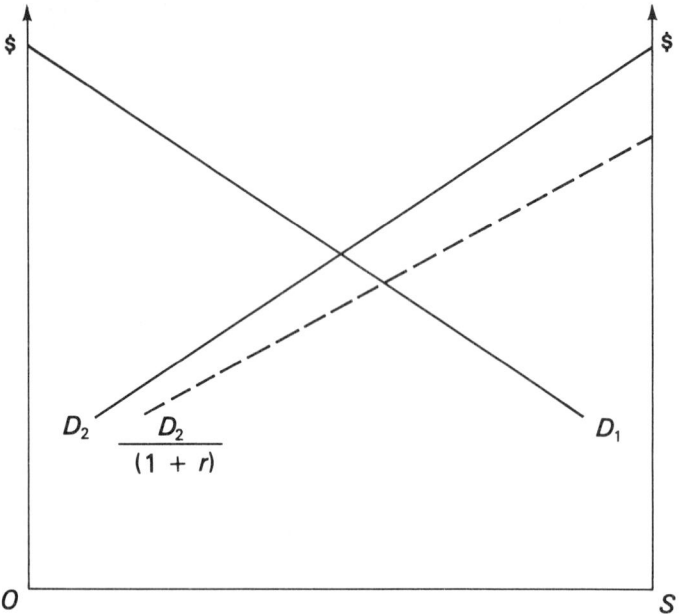

Figure 10.1

Question 9 What is:

        (a) the marginal user cost schedule?
        (b) the marginal cost schedule?

Question 10 When the market is in equilibrium, then

$$P_1 = \frac{P_2}{(1 + r)}$$

On Figure 10.1 show how much oil is sold in Periods 1 and 2, and at what prices.

Question 11 If the discount rate is 10 per cent and $P_1 = \$20$, what is P_2?

Question 12 Suppose that producers adopt a higher discount rate than that implied in Figure 10.1; would more or less oil be sold in Period 1?

So far we have assumed that producers sell their oil in a perfectly competitive market. We now consider what difference it would make if all oil stocks were owned by one producer.

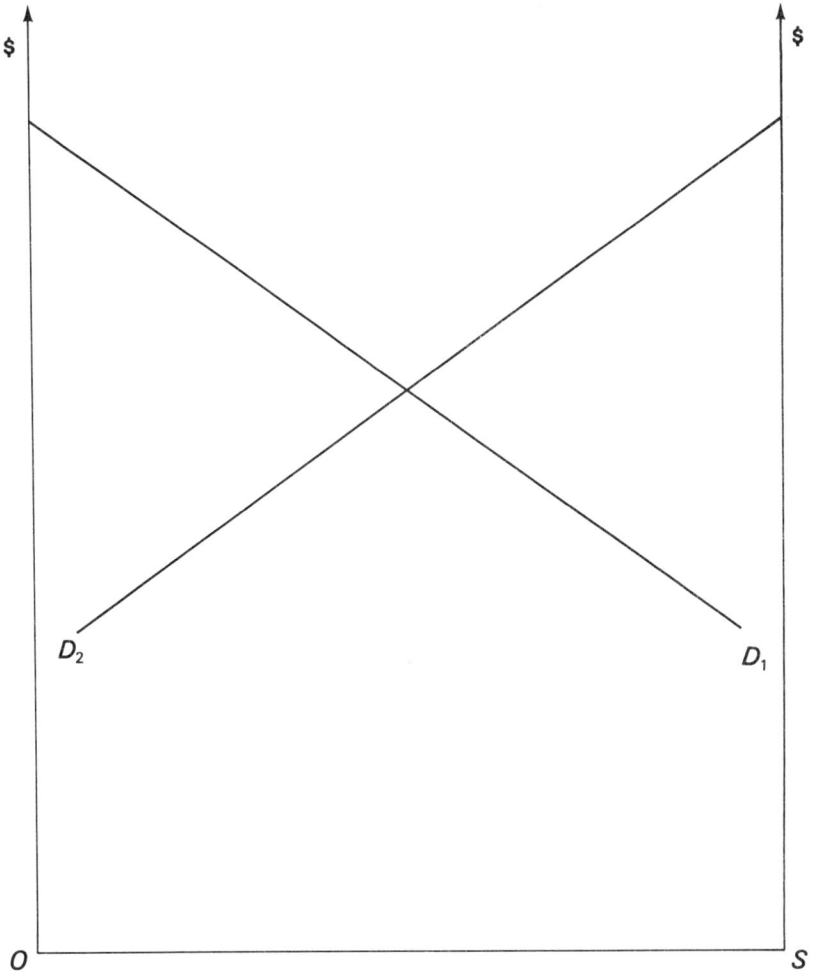

Figure 10.2

Question 13 What is the monopolist's equilibrium condition for long-run profit maximisation?

Question 14 Figure 10.1 has been produced in Figure 10.2. Show the monopolist's output and prices in the two periods and compare these with those of the competitive market. (You will need to complete the diagram by drawing in appropriate schedules as we have only drawn the demand curves for both periods.)

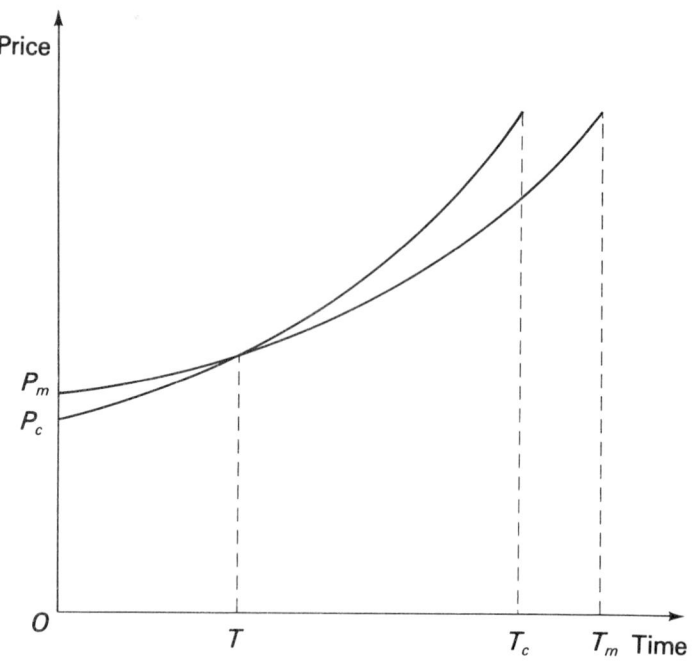

Figure 10.3

Question 15 (a) Is the monopolist's price higher or lower than the competitive price in Period 1? Why is this?

   (b) What about his price in Period 2? Explain the difference.

   With linear demand curves, as we have drawn in Figures 10.1 and 10.2, the price paths over time will differ for monopoly and competition. (If the demand curves were iso-elastic, then the competitive and monopoly price paths would coincide.) With competition the initial price (P_c) is lower than the monopoly price (P_m); this encourages more rapid use of the oil and the stock will be depleted sooner than would be the case under monopoly. This is shown in Figure 10.3 where T_c is the time when oil resources will be exhausted under perfect competition.

Question 16 Examining Figure 10.3 you see that the initial price is higher under monopoly but after time T, prices will be lower under monopoly than under competition. Can you explain why this should be?

Question 17 When you answered Question 5 your answer depended, among other things, on the rate of discount you adopted. What rate did you use? What rate do you think a producer would choose? Why? Do you think the rate will be the same for all producers?

We now examine the implications of relaxing the other assumptions we made on page 99. We start by considering factors influencing the demand for oil and after that we turn to those affecting supply.

Question 18 In Figures 10.1 and 10.2 the demand curves for the two periods are shown as identical. Would you expect the long-run own price elasticity of demand to be the same as in the short run? Explain your answer.

Question 19 Suppose that in the current period, producers' expectations of future demand change. What effect would this have on the equilibrium price path if they now expect that:

   (a) long-run demand is more elastic than short-run?
   (b) the recession is ending and the world economy is picking up?

We have seen that changes in producers' expectations about future demand will affect their production decisions, that is to say the rate at which they deplete their stock. In equilibrium, as we saw, net revenue in the current period will equal discounted net revenue in future periods if producers maximise profits. Thus, any factors which affect the *user cost* in different periods will affect the equilibrium price path.

Question 20 Before you read on, think what might affect user costs (other than changes in demand).

In our simple two-period model we assumed that the size of oil reserves was known.[2]

---

2. The size of known and potential oil reserves is the subject of a large number of studies (for brief discussion, see Fesharaki and Isaak, 1983, Ch. 1). We assume here that we are considering 'proven reserves', that is to say oil that can be extracted with current technology, costs and prices.

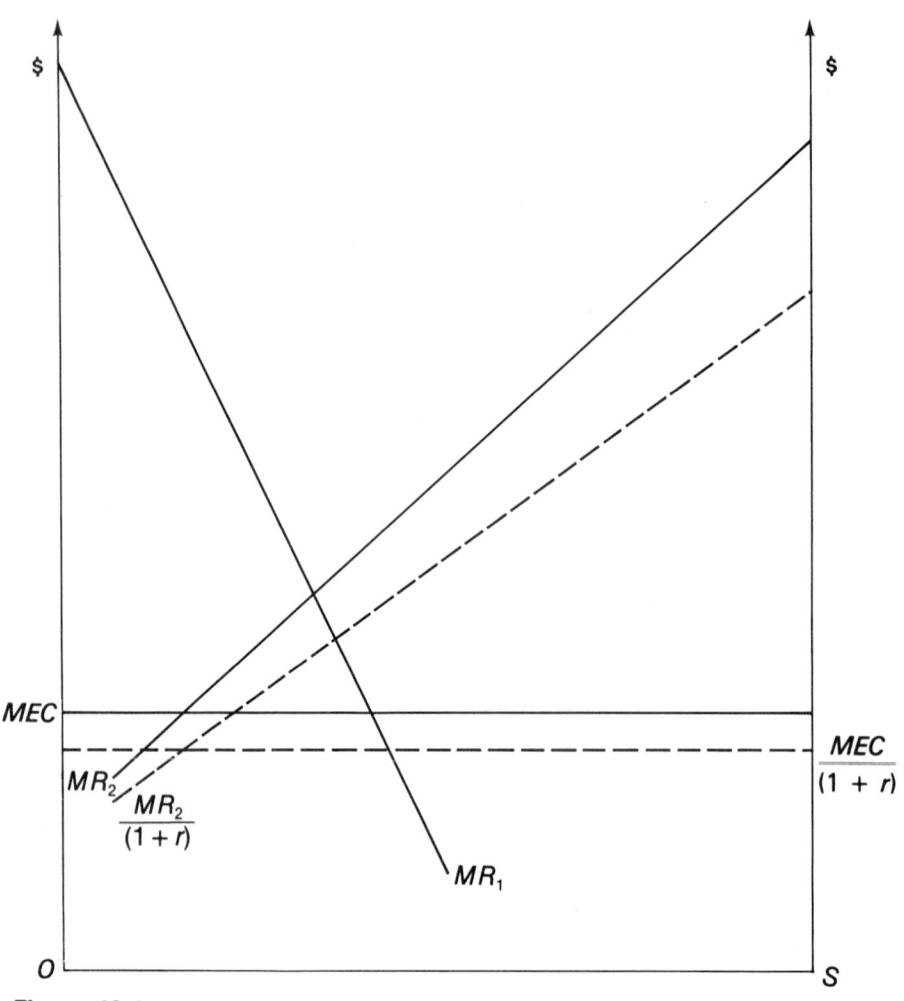

Figure 10.4

Question 21 If new oil reserves are now discovered and this discovery is unexpected, what happens to prices in Periods 1 and 2 (assuming that nothing else changes)? Does it make any difference whether you take the perfectly competitive or the monopoly case?

Question 22 If the discovery were not totally unexpected, what difference would it make?

We started by assuming that marginal extraction costs were zero. Now we must see what difference it will make if they are positive.

Question 23 How do we find the marginal user cost? (If you cannot answer this question, go back to the beginning of the exercise.)

Question 24 How do we obtain the marginal cost curve?

In Figure 10.4, which illustrates the monopoly case (we have not shown the demand curves in order to avoid an unnecessarily complicated diagram), we introduce positive marginal extraction costs and assume that these are the same in both periods.

Question 25 Draw the marginal user cost and marginal cost schedules on Figure 10.4.

Question 26 How much oil will be sold in the first period? How does this compare with the case where there were no extraction costs? Explain the difference.

Question 27 Check that:

$$MR_1 - MEC = \frac{MR_2 - MEC}{(1 + r)}$$

Question 28 Suppose that the marginal extraction cost were to fall in Period 2 because of some technological innovation in extraction methods. What would happen to prices?

Earlier when discussing factors influencing the elasticity of demand (see Question 18), you considered the availability of substitute sources of energy.

Question 29 What are the possible substitutes for oil? Are these substitutes equally suitable for all current uses of oil? Are they also exhaustible?

With current knowledge, some alternative sources of energy are very expensive and thus not extensively exploited (e.g. nuclear fission). As reserves of oil are run down over time, oil prices rise and these higher prices will make currently unattractive sources of energy (and oil) viable. There are vast quantities of oil available in shale and tar sands but at today's oil prices this source of oil is not worth exploiting. However, as oil fields run out, producers will turn to alternative sources and the existence of such a backstop

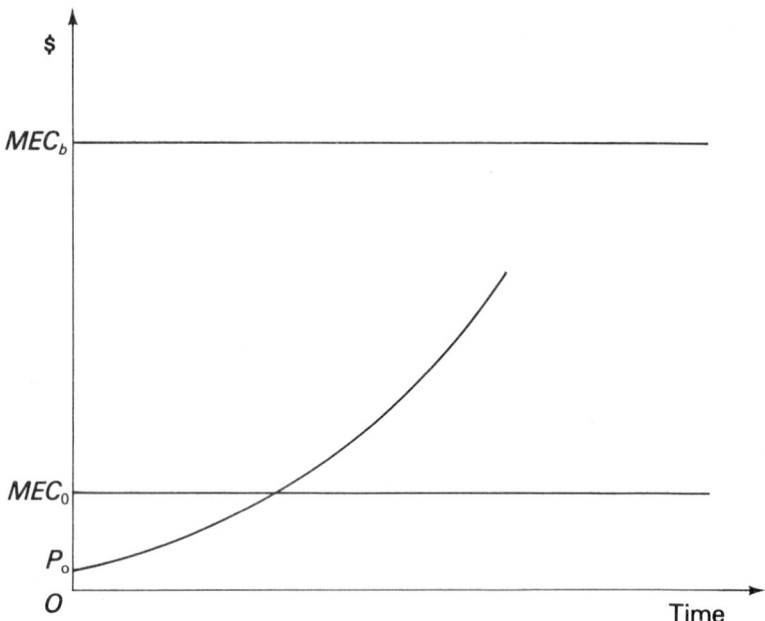

Figure 10.5

technology' means that oil prices cannot be sustained above the level at which the backstop fuel can be marketed.[3]

If the source of a backstop is virtually unlimited (or if fuel is available from renewable sources such as wind, tide or sun), the market will be perfectly competitive. In Figure 10.5 we simplify the situation by assuming that marginal extraction costs of oil fields are constant at MEC_0 and that the marginal extraction cost of the backstop fuel is MEC_b. The equilibrium price path of *unextracted* oil from oil fields is shown starting at P_0.

Question 30 Draw in the price path of *extracted* oil. Assuming that this represents the price path achieved under perfect competition, would we begin to exploit backstop fuel resources at an earlier or later date if the oil industry were a monopoly?

Question 31 There is uncertainty over the price at which backstop fuels will become available. What other major sources of uncertainty do producers face when choosing their depletion rate? Summarise them before continuing.

3. For discussion of the price at which such backstop fuel becomes competitive, see Ericsson and Morgan 1978.

Question 32 Throughout our analysis we have concentrated on the equilibrium price path for oil. As we have seen, *ceteris paribus*, market forces will cause it to rise over time. However, if we were to trace oil prices over the last fifty years, we should not expect to find a steady increase. Why not?

We have also seen that if oil is sold on a competitive market, reserves will be used up faster than under a monopoly, even if the rate of discount were the same for both types of market. Before we finish this part of our analysis of oil prices, we consider briefly whether we are using up oil at too fast a rate. In assessing whether the rate is too fast or not, we are concerned with a question of equity: if we continue to consume oil at our existing rate, is this fair on future generations? The higher the rate of discount we adopt, the quicker we use up the stocks of oil; if we choose a low rate, then we leave more for future generations.

Question 33 What determines the choice of the discount rate by market producers? If all oil stocks are owned by countries, then it is these countries which can choose the rate of discount. Will this be the same as the market rate and, in fairness to future members of society, should it be?

Question 34 (a) If you are promised £100 today or an amount giving you the *same* purchasing power in a year's time, will you be indifferent as to the timing of these sums? If not, why not?
(b) Now try to consider the question from the point of view of a *country*. If *you* are not indifferent, does it follow that any society will also not be indifferent? If so, will the reasons be the same as you advanced to support your choice?

The choice of an appropriate discount rate is clearly important in determining how rapidly resources are depleted, and there are various reasons why society might wish to use a different rate from that adopted in the market. If you are interested in exploring the choice of an optimal depletion rate, you could start by reading articles by Heal (1975, 1981) or by Kay and Mirrlees (1975) which provide excellent introductions to some of the issues.

All the material contained in this exercise is covered comprehensively by Dasgupta and Heal (1979) but you may find it rather heavy going. Solow (1974) provides a useful overview of the main issues, while an excellent introduction to the theory in this part of the exercise, and also to that dealt with in the next part, can be found in Chapter 1 of Griffin and Teece (1982). Finally, an article by Mead (1982) applies this theory to oil prices in the 1970s and provides a good link with the subject matter of the second part of the exercise, i.e. OPEC's pricing policies.

References

Danielsen, Albert L. (1982) *The Evolution of OPEC*, Harcourt Brace Jovanovich.

Dasgupta, P.A. and Heal, G.M. (1979) *Economic Theory and Exhaustible Resources*, Cambridge University Press.

Ericsson, Neil R. and Morgan, Peter (1978) 'The economic feasibility of shale oil: an activity analysis', *Bell Journal of Economics*, 9, pp. 457—487.

Fesharaki, Fereidun and Isaak, David T. (1983) *OPEC, the Gulf, and the World Petroleum Market*, Croom Helm.

*Griffin, J.M. and Teece, D.J. (1982) *OPEC Behavior and World Oil Prices*, George Allen and Unwin.

Heal, G.M. (1975) 'Economic aspects of natural resource depletion', in D.W. Pearce and J. Rose (eds.), *The Economics of Natural Resource Depletion*, Macmillan.

Heal, G.M. (1981) 'Economics and resources', in J.A. Butlin (ed.), *Economics and Resources Policy*, Longman.

Kay, J.A. and Mirrlees, J.A. (1975) 'The desirability of natural resource depletion', in D.W. Pearce and J. Rose (eds.), *The Economics of Natural Resource Depletion*, Macmillan.

*Mead, W.J. (1982) 'An economic analysis of crude oil behavior in the 1970s', in Ragaei El Mallakh (ed.), *OPEC: Twenty Years and Beyond*, Croom Helm.

*Solow, Robert M. (1974) 'The economics of resources or the resources of economics', *American Economic Review*, 64, May, pp. 1—14.

---

*Suggested supplementary reading.

11

OPEC – The Conservationists' Friend? Part II

OPEC is probably the best known of all cartels. However, not all producers are members of OPEC, so how does OPEC decide what price to charge for its oil, given the presence of a competitive fringe of other oil producers? Once the price has been set, can OPEC ensure that none of its members cheat by selling more than their agreed quota? These are the questions we discuss in Problem 11. In order to tackle them you need to know something about OPEC's history and membership. Background material on this and on recent developments in the oil market has been provided and it might be a good idea to read to the end of the problem before you start to work through the questions. In addition, you need to understand the following:

(a) oligopoly and strategic behaviour;
(b) the conditions for joint profit maximisation by a cartel;
(c) how price is determined in the dominant-firm leadership model;
(d) barriers to entry and limit pricing;
(e) the goal of an oligopolist.

Some Background Material[1]

OPEC was set up in 1960 by the five major oil exporting countries: Saudi Arabia, Iran, Iraq, Kuwait and Venezuela. Its stated objectives are outlined below:

(1) The principal aim of the organisation shall be the co-ordination and unification of the petroleum policies of

---

1. A concise introduction can be found in Griffin and Teece (1982), Ch. 1. For a more complete account the reader is referred to Allen (1979) and Danielsen (1982).

member countries and the determination of the best
means of safeguarding their interests, individually and
collectively.
(2) The organisation shall devise ways and means of ensur-
ing the stabilisation of prices ... (and) eliminating harm-
ful and unnecessary fluctuations.

(OPEC 1976, *The Structure of the Organisation of the
Petroleum Exporting Countries*, OPEC, Vienna, quoted
by Johany (1980), p. 6.)

In the years leading up to 1960, oil-producing countries had found
themselves increasingly at odds with the international oil companies which
extracted oil under concessionary agreements and which made all decisions
on output levels. The terms of these agreements varied somewhat but all
involved the payment of royalties per barrel or ton. In the late 1940s,
Venezuela became the first country to introduce a system of profit-sharing:
in addition to the traditional royalty, it received one-half of the difference
between the selling price and the production costs. Consequently companies
operating in Venezuela found it less profitable to extract oil there and they
switched their activities to the Middle East where profit-sharing had not yet
been introduced. By the early 1950s, however, profit-sharing became the
general rule.

The first country to nationalise an oil company was Iran (in 1951); other
countries took some time to follow suit. In 1968, OPEC declared that it
aimed to maximise oil revenues and to gain control of the oil company
operations, but it was only in October 1973 that ownership was effectively
transferred, with OPEC countries making the decision as to how much oil to
produce. The closure of the Suez Canal in 1967 (not to reopen until 1975) and
the Biafran war in Nigeria meant that supply was reduced and the cost of
transporting oil from Middle Eastern fields rose. Libyan oil became sought
after by European buyers and, in order to extract higher royalties from oil
companies, Colonel Ghaddafi instructed companies operating in Libya to
reduce output in 1970. Coinciding with Algerian nationalisation of oil, this
led Middle Eastern countries to increase pressure for more favourable terms
and ultimately to take control. During this time, membership of OPEC had
been rising and it reached its full thirteen members when Gabon joined in
1975. The market price of oil was already rising when the outbreak of the
(fourth) Arab—Israeli war in October 1973 was followed by an OPEC
embargo and a large increase in the OPEC marker price early in 1974. The
embargo and accompanying production cuts ended after six months and no
similar leap in OPEC prices occurred until autumn 1978 when the political
unrest in Iran led to Iranian exports being suspended at the turn of the year.
Although exports were resumed, at a lower level, three months later, Rotter-
dam spot prices continued at higher levels than the OPEC marker price
which had also risen sharply. The outbreak of the Iran—Iraq war in 1980

Table 11.1 Estimated Production of Oil (1000 barrels per day)

	1972	1973	1974	1975	1976	1977	1978	1979	1980	1981	1982	1983	1984
OPEC:													
Indonesia	1,027	1,300	1,457	1,300	1,500	1,690	1,650	1,600	1,570	1,607	1,341	1,292	1,332
Iran	4,900	6,000	6,128	5,600	5,875	5,650	5,250	2,900	1,280	1,375	1,896	2,606	2,166
Iraq	1,500	1,882	1,829	2,400	2,070	2,150	2,500	3,370	2,600	892	914	905	1,218
Kuwait	2,750	2,890	2,600	1,950	1,820	1,700	1,900	2,210	1,400	916	675	912	925
Qatar	450	556	546	410	485	350	480	480	470	414	340	270	404
Saudi Arabia	5,255	7,418	8,400	7,000	8,570	8,950	7,800	9,250	9,620	9,642	6,484	4,872	4,545
UAE	1,130	1,509	1,987	1,800	1,945	2,030	1,834	1,825	1,740	1,512	1,247	1,119	1,142
Algeria	1,061	1,035	889	935	950	990	1,260	1,240	1,000	750	750	687	608
Gabon	125	145	182	200	220	225	170	192	145	147	130	150	150
Libya	2,230	2,117	1,700	1,400	1,900	2,050	2,050	2,050	1,780	1,063	1,127	1,020	1,090
Nigeria	1,800	2,000	2,300	1,850	2,020	2,150	1,800	2,370	2,100	1,369	1,324	1,232	1,414
Ecuador	59	197	232	165	185	180	200	220	230	204	215	236	254
Venezuela	3,200	3,370	3,025	2,400	2,290	2,280	2,150	2,330	2,150	2,093	1,826	1,791	1,724
Total OPEC	25,487	30,419	31,275	27,410	29,830	30,395	29,044	30,037	26,085	21,984	18,269	17,092	16,972
Other non-Communist	15,302	15,482	15,107	14,691	15,021	15,983	17,139	18,411	19,009	19,292	20,083	21,222	22,148
incl. Mexico	440	478	514	710	850	990	1,270	1,490	1,960	2,390	2,734	2,702	2,743
USA	9,500	9,225	8,945	8,370	8,105	8,240	8,660	8,650	8,650	8,588	8,655	8,669	8,750
Norway	34	38	30	170	300	270	350	390	530	508	488	600	688
UK	2	2	2	40	230	775	1,100	1,570	1,600	1,790	2,050	2,260	2,452
Total non-Communist world	40,789	45,901	46,382	42,101	44,851	46,378	46,183	48,448	45,094	41,276	38,352	38,314	39,120

Source: Oil and Gas Journal.

might have been expected to lead to further increases in OPEC prices, but the recession in the Western world has checked the trend and the current problem facing OPEC is how to prevent the price of oil from falling.

Before tackling the rest of this exercise, have a look at Table 11.1 which shows oil output figures for the non-Communist world.

Question 1 It is generally advantageous for sellers to combine to raise the price of their product. What conditions facilitate the formation of a cartel?

Question 2 Are any of these conditions to be found in the oil market?

Question 3 (a) Suppose, for the moment, that oil is found only in countries of OPEC members (i.e. there is no competitive fringe). If all producers decided to act jointly to maximise OPEC profits, what would they have to do to achieve this?
(b) Would it be necessary to arrange to share out the profits?
(c) Why does the existence of a competitive fringe prevent OPEC from acting this way?

The cartel model most favoured by economists analysing the oil market is one where OPEC acts as a dominant producer or price-leader.

Question 4 (a) What conditions are necessary to enable OPEC to take on the role of price-leader?
(b) How would a cartel operating this way set its price? What factors would it consider?
(c) Is the demand curve facing the cartel more or less elastic than the world demand curve?
(d) If demand falls, due to recession, would OPEC adjust its output?

Question 5 What was OPEC's market share in 1973, 1978 and 1984?

Question 6 We continue with the price-leader model but take a *hypothetical* case.
(a) Find the profit-maximising price for 'OPEC' by completing Figure 11.1(b), given the information on non-OPEC supply and world demand shown in Figure 11.1(a).

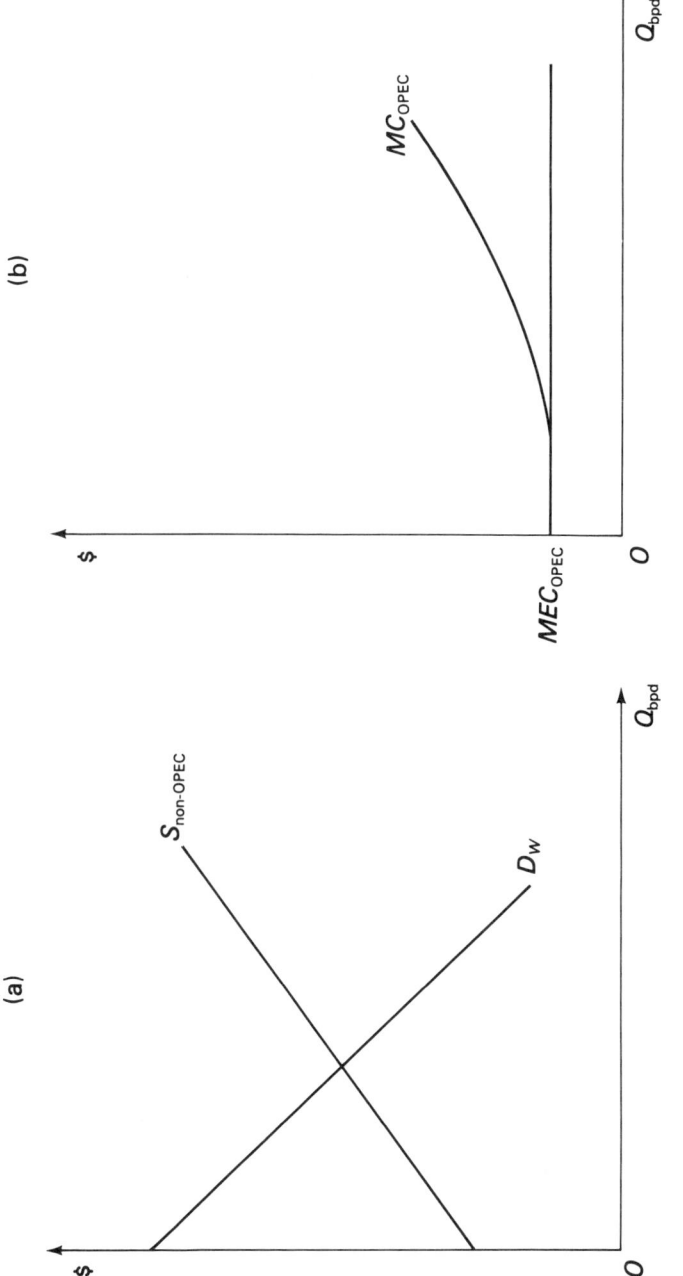

Figure 11.1

(b) In such a case as this, would it be possible for OPEC to set a price such that it could exclude all other producers from the market?

Question 7 (a) An established firm in an industry may set its price with a view to preventing entry by other firms. Such a price is called a limit price. Can you think what factors are likely to determine the level of such a price?
(b) Has this concept any relevance for OPEC?

All cartels face the problem of how to maintain their chosen price above the competitive level. Only if all members of the cartel are happy with their market share (or revenue) will this be straightforward. The pricing system OPEC adopted in the 1970s consisted of setting a marker price for Saudi Arabian crude and leaving other members to set their own prices. Oil varies in quality and members set their prices by reference to the marker price so as to reflect these differences and differences in transport costs. Refineries enter into contracts of one year or more with OPEC countries and purchase the mix of qualities that maximise their profits. Oil buyers thus determined the total output of OPEC. Any OPEC member, dissatisfied with its market share, could adjust its price. Ignoring transport costs, oils of similar quality would generally be priced similarly and thus a small change in price could result in a large change in sales. Though oil refineries purchase from OPEC on long-term contracts, they can also trade on the spot markets where prices vary from day to day, unlike OPEC prices which are changed at intervals following meetings of OPEC members.

Question 8 The existence of spot market trading puts strains on OPEC's differential pricing system. Why?

Question 9 When spot market prices rise, OPEC prices also rise. Can you explain why?

The problems of the OPEC relative value pricing system became acute with the world recession, and since 1982 OPEC has agreed to limit output and allocate production quotas in order to maintain its pricing structure.

Question 10 By how much has OPEC cut its production? How much has Saudi Arabia's output fallen over the same period?

As might be expected, OPEC has found it easier to agree on the overall production ceiling than to settle the quotas amongst members. In general Saudi Arabia bore the brunt of production cuts, but in October 1984, when

OPEC decided to cut production by 1.5 million barrels to achieve a total production level of 16 million barrels per day, Saudi Arabia made it plain it was not prepared to continue to take the major share of the cuts as it was already producing only 3.5 million barrels per day out of its allowed quota of 5 million. This October 1984 meeting was also unusual in that delegates from non-OPEC countries attended the meeting and one of these, Mexico, indicated that it would cut output by ten per cent (see reports in *The Times*, 29 to 31 October 1984). The presence of Mexico is interesting as Mexico is likely to become a major producer of oil in the next few years (see Noreng 1982; also Pindyck 1982).

Question 11 Do you think that Mexico will maintain this cut if OPEC members continue to cheat?

Question 12 Under what circumstances might OPEC members try to cheat? Would it be easier for some members to cheat and not to be detected than it would for others? Why is it that Nigeria is frequently cited as an offending member?

Question 13 If other members cheat, do you think that Saudi Arabia will continue to refuse to cut its production?

Question 14 Would the existence of spot markets affect the likelihood of OPEC members cheating?

Question 15 Do you think that non-OPEC members find OPEC activities beneficial? What factors are likely to influence the state-owned British National Oil Corporation (BNOC) when setting an official price for North Sea oil?

The production ceiling of 16 million barrels per day agreed by OPEC in October 1984 is considerably less than current OPEC productive capacity and the market was sceptical of OPEC's ability to maintain output at this level. The continued weakening of the spot market and cheating among members led OPEC to announce a new disciplinary code at its meeting at the end of 1984. A monitoring scheme is to be introduced and 'independent inspectors will have full access to production records, delivery schedules and price arrangements' for each member country (*The Times*, 29 December 1984). At the same time, relative prices were changed with heavy crudes rising by 50 cents a barrel and light crudes falling by 25 cents, leaving the marker price at $29. (Significantly, Nigeria and Algeria opted out of the agreement.) No announcement was made about possible sanctions against any members who cheated. The OPEC President said that 'the prospect of public embarrassment within OPEC would be enough to deter breaches of the disciplinary code' (*The Times*, 28 December 1984).

Question 16 What kind of sanctions could OPEC employ?

Osborne (1976) has suggested that one possible strategy a cartel could adopt to reduce cheating is that of maintaining market shares by retaliating whenever a member cheats. If one member increases output, by, say, 10 per cent, then other members should also increase their output by 10 per cent. In this way, market shares within the cartel would be maintained and the cheating member is forced to share in the losses his action has imposed on the cartel group. You may be interested to read Osborne's article; if you do, consider carefully whether conditions within OPEC are such that adoption of such a rule is feasible and whether it would be beneficial to cartel members. When you have done this, read Holahan (1978) and Rothschild (1981).

Question 17 There are various types of cartel but the unifying feature is that they all aim to maintain a product price above the competitive level by restricting output. As recent developments within OPEC show, this is not always an easy task. During the 1970s the problem of output quotas in OPEC was not so acute. Why was this?

Some commentators have argued that judged on its performance in the 1970s OPEC could not be considered to be a cartel and that price rises can be explained in other ways. If you read Mead's article after completing Part I, you will have already come across Johany's discussion of the 1973/74 price rise where he argues that it can be explained by the change in property rights from oil companies to oil countries (see Mead 1982, Johany 1980 or 1982).

Question 18 Can you remember Johany's analysis, as set out by Mead?
  (*Hint:* he suggests that the oil companies adopted a higher discount rate than OPEC countries would have chosen. What reasons did he give to support this view? Even if you did not read Mead, you might still like to think about this point.)

Teece (1982) argues that OPEC members do not maximise wealth but instead they determine output levels so as to obtain revenues sufficient to cover their investment needs. This target revenue hypothesis implies that the OPEC supply curve might be backward sloping where investment possibilities are limited in member countries. From a 1985 perspective, much of this debate is irrelevant: OPEC is certainly behaving like a cartel now. However, OPEC's objectives in determining output levels merit consideration and if you wish to follow up on this aspect, you might start by reading Chapters 2 to 4 in Griffin and Teece (1982).

A great deal has been published on OPEC. A useful basic reference on conditions favouring the formation of cartels is Scherer (1980). Gilbert (1978) and Newbery (1981) analyse OPEC's pricing policy given the existence of the competitive fringe. Price forecasts in earlier studies have been overtaken by events since the Iranian revolution; nevertheless you will find much to interest you in articles by Cremer and Weitzman (1976), Hnyilicza and Pindyck (1976), and Pindyck (1978). More up-to-date studies include Pindyck (1982) and Choe (1984).

References

Allen, Loring (1979) *OPEC Oil*, Oelgeschlager, Gunn and Hain.
Choe, B-J. (1984) *A Model of World Energy Markets and OPEC Pricing*, World Bank Staff Working Papers No. 633, World Bank.
Cremer, J. and Weitzman, M.L. (1976) 'OPEC and the monopoly price of world oil', *European Economic Review*, 8, pp. 155—164.
Danielsen, Albert L. (1982) *The Evolution of OPEC*, Harcourt Brace Jovanovich.
El Mallakh, Ragaei (ed.) (1982) *OPEC: Twenty Years and Beyond*, Croom Helm.
Gilbert, R.J. (1978) 'Dominant firm pricing in a market for an exhaustible resource', *Bell Journal of Economics*, 9, pp. 385—395.
Griffin, James M. and Teece, David J. (1982) *OPEC Behavior and World Oil Prices*, George Allen and Unwin.
Hnyilicza, E. and Pindyck, R.S. (1976) 'Pricing policies for a two-part exhaustible resource cartel: the case of OPEC', *European Economic Review*, 8, pp. 139—154.
*Holahan, W.L. (1978) 'Cartel problems: comment', *American Economic Review*, 68, pp. 942—946.
Johany, Ali D. (1980) *'The Myth of the OPEC Cartel'*, John Wiley.
Johany, Ali D. (1982) 'OPEC and the price of oil: cartelization or alteration of property rights', in Ragaei El Mallakh (ed.), op. cit.
Mead, Walter J. (1982) 'An economic analysis of crude oil price behavior in the 1970s', in Ragaei El Mallakh (ed.), op. cit.
Newbery, D.M.G. (1981) 'Oil prices, cartels, and the problem of dynamic inconsistency', *Economic Journal*, 91, pp. 617—646.
Noreng, Øystein (1982) 'Friends or fellow travellers? The relationship of non-OPEC exporters with OPEC', in Ragaei El Mallakh (ed.), op. cit.
*Osborne, D.K. (1976) 'Cartel problems', *American Economic Review*, 66, pp. 835—844.
Pindyck, R.S. (1978) 'Gains to producers from the cartelization of exhaustible resources', *Review of Economics and Statistics*, 60, pp. 238—251.
Pindyck, R.S. (1982) 'Some long-term problems in OPEC oil pricing', in Ragaei El Mallakh (ed.), op. cit.
Rothschild, R. (1981) 'Cartel problems: note', American Economic Review, 71, pp. 179—181.

*Scherer, F. (1980) *Industrial Market Structure and Economic Performance*, Rand McNally, 2nd ed., Chapter 7.

Teece, David J. (1982) 'OPEC behaviour: an alternative view', in James M. Griffin and David J. Teece (eds.), op. cit.

---

*Suggested supplementary reading.

12

Choose Your Partners

There are many different types of firms: multinationals, large business corporations, small family businesses, labour managed co-operatives. In this problem we compare the typical entrepreneurial firm of the textbook with a partnership such as you observe for many small firms of accountants or lawyers. In our problem, all the profits of the partnership are shared equally between the partners and we ask what difference it makes if a good or service is produced by such a partnership instead of a firm owned by one person. Will the two types of firm produce the same level of output? In the short-run, will they employ the same quantity of factor inputs? Before you start work, revise the following:

(a) the role of the entrepreneur;
(b) the goal of the firm;
(c) total, average and marginal product;
(d) the law of diminishing returns;
(e) marginal value product;
(f) derivation of the conditions for profit maximisation.

Suppose the time is a few years hence and several of you have set up in business together as economic consultants. Business has been good and you are just about to hold a meeting to decide whether to take on additional partner(s). Before attending that meeting, take a little time to decide whether you will favour expansion.

The current situation is as follows:

(i) you can sell your services (X) at a given price (P), i.e. the market is competitive;

(ii) secretarial assistance (S) is hired at the market wage (m);

(iii) you rent capital (K) at the market rate (r) (what capital might you need?);

119

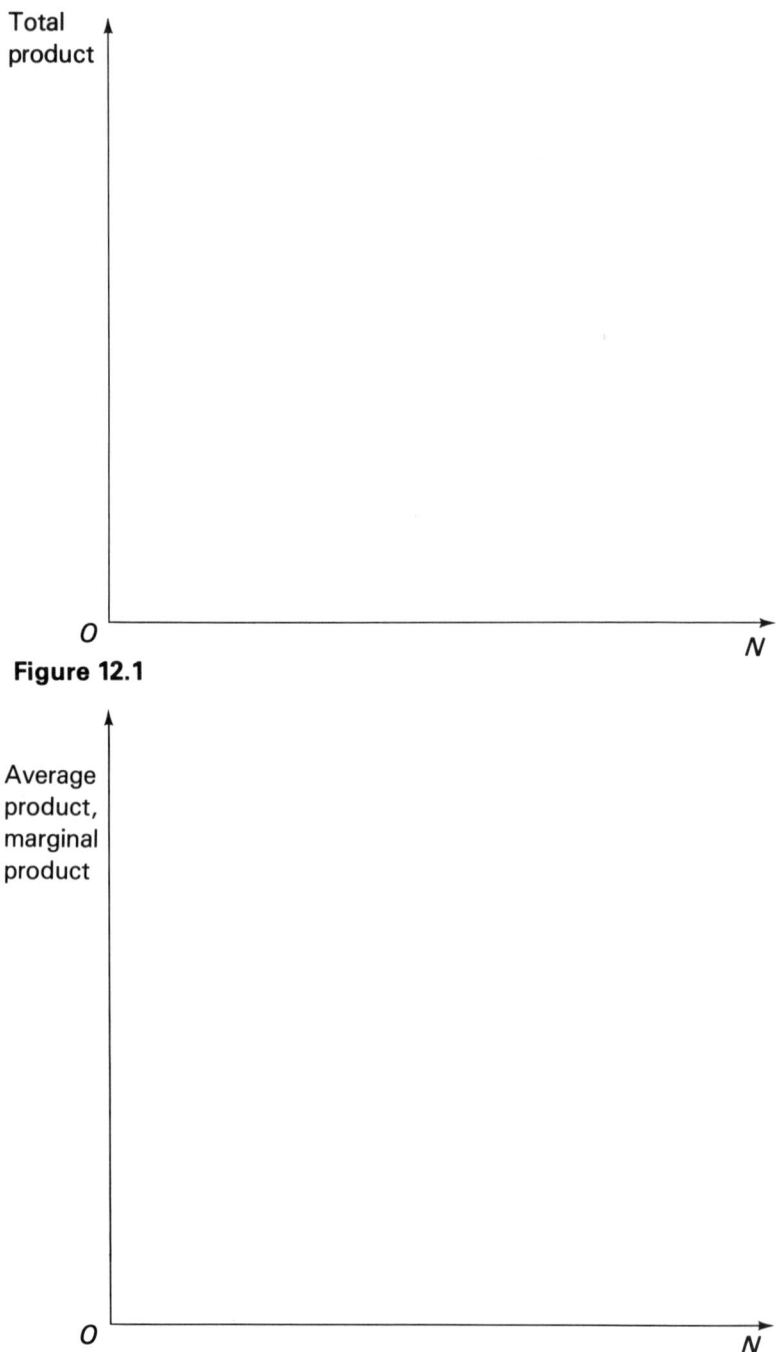

Figure 12.1

Figure 12.2

(iv) you and your partners (N = number of partners) each work a forty hour week and divide up any surplus (V) equally between you. In other words, you all receive the same income, $Y = V/N$;

(v) for simplicity, assume that you have no materials or other non-labour variable costs.

Question 1 Your production function is:

$$X = f(N, S, K)$$

(a) Assuming that S and K are fixed, draw a curve to represent the total product schedule of economists on Figure 12.1.

(b) Explain its shape.

Question 2 (a) How do you find the marginal physical product of a partner (X_N)? Is $X_N \gtreqless 0$? What about X_{NN}?

(b) How do you find the average product (X/N)?

(c) Draw the appropriate marginal and average product curves on Figure 12.2, taking care to relate these curves to the total product schedule you drew in Figure 12.1.

Question 3 (a) Assuming that your aim is to maximise your income (Y), write out your objective function.

(b) Continue to assume that S and K are fixed. What is the condition determining the optimal number of partners? Explain in words.

Question 4 When S and K are fixed, then fixed costs (F) = $mS + rK$, and we can write

$$Y = \frac{PX - F}{N}$$

On Figure 12.3, draw a curve that plots Y as N increases. What determines the shape of this curve?

(*Hint*: how is it related to earlier diagrams? Start by thinking about PX, bearing in mind that S and K are fixed and only N varies.)

Figure 12.3

Question 5 Now draw in a schedule for the value of the marginal product (PX_N). Why does it cut the net average revenue schedule (NAR_N) at its maximum?

Question 6 Suppose that the current market wage of economists is w_0, and your firm faces a perfectly elastic supply schedule as shown on Figure 12.4.

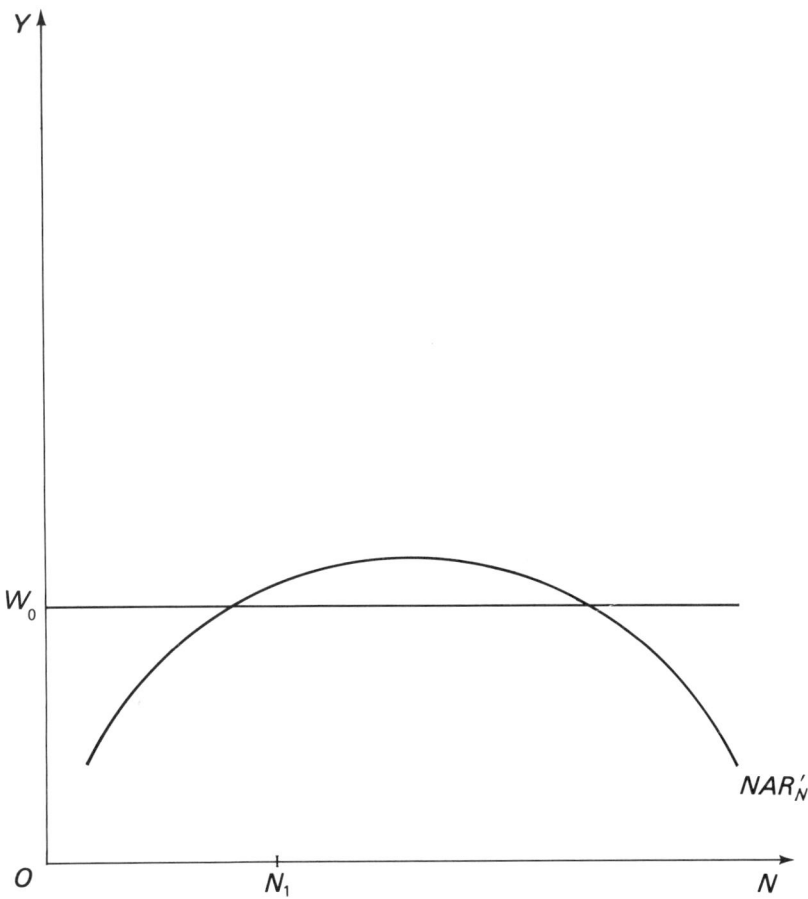

Figure 12.4

(a) If the current number of partners in your firm is N_1, what is your current income?

(b) Will you take on additional *partners*? If so, how many and what will happen to your income?

Question 7 (a) Suppose you own the firm and that *you employ* economists instead of taking them on as partners. Assuming that you aim to maximise your income, how many will you hire? Show this on Figure 12.4.

(b) Why is it that these two types of firm (entrepreneural and partnership) do not employ the same number of economists?

(c) Will both types of firm provide the same quantity of service?

Question 8 We have assumed that S and K are fixed, but we need to ask how much S and K should be employed. When the firm is a partnership, write out the first order equilibrium conditions for N, S and K. (You already have the condition for N.)

$$\frac{\partial Y}{\partial N} =$$

$$\frac{\partial Y}{\partial S} =$$

$$\frac{\partial Y}{\partial K} =$$

Question 9 Now write out the first order equilibrium conditions, assuming that the firm is an entrepreneurial firm with you as the owner.

$$\frac{\partial V}{\partial N} =$$

$$\frac{\partial V}{\partial S} =$$

$$\frac{\partial V}{\partial K} =$$

Question 10 Do the two firms hire the same amounts of S and K? Explain your answer.

Question 11 We now explore further the differences between a partnership and an entrepreneurial firm in the short run, i.e. we assume that S and K are fixed.

Figure 12.5

(a) What would happen if a lump-sum tax were imposed on the firm? Show the outcome on Figure 12.5.
(b) What happens to N and to X?
(c) Is this what would happen in an entrepreneurial firm? Explain.

Figure 12.6

Question 12 Now repeat the analysis of Question 11 but, this time, consider a rise in the price of the service you provide. Use Figure 12.6 to illustrate the outcome for the partnership.

Up until now we have considered a perfectly elastic supply curve for economists. Suppose, however, that your partnership faces an upward-sloping supply schedule, *BB'*, as shown in Figure 12.7.

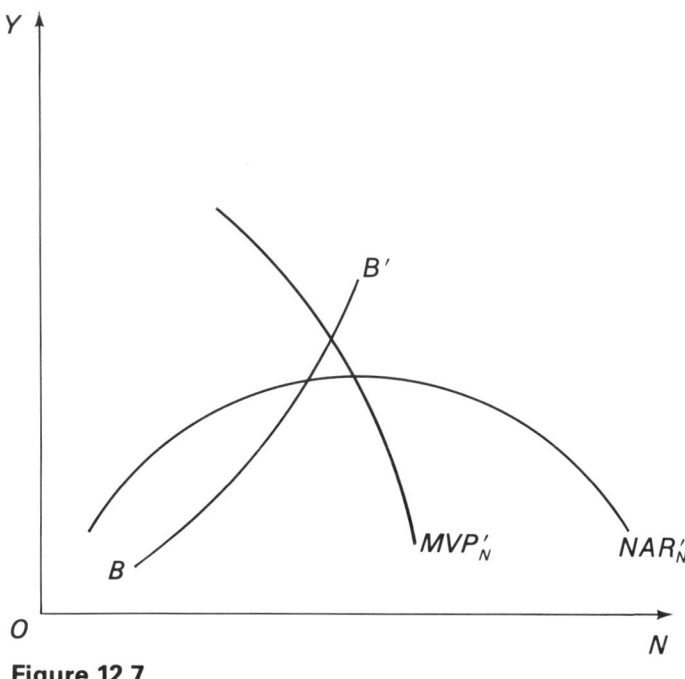

Figure 12.7

Question 13 (a) How many economists would you take into partnership?
(b) If a lump-sum tax were imposed, would the optimal
number of economists change? Compare your answer
with that you gave to Question 11.

As we have seen, changes in the business conditions you face may result in
your firm wishing to shed partners. This result, while rational within the
terms of the model as set out here,[1] does seem at variance with what we
observe. Partners, once admitted, do not generally leave when business
improves unless they are compensated or can find more lucrative partnerships elsewhere.

---

1. This result may not follow when we make other assumptions, e.g. that the firm produces
more than one product, or that the partners maximise utility functions which contain arguments
in addition to that of income maximisation.

Meade suggests that partnerships may adopt rules so that new partner(s) wishing to enter may join only if existing partners agree and that no partner can be forced to leave against her will. Moreover, if any partner should wish to leave, she may do so only with the agreement of remaining partners (1972, p. 421).

Question 14 Suppose that as a result of a price increase, the partnership wishes to reduce its numbers, currently at N_2, as shown in Figure 12.8, and (given these rules) can only persuade partners to leave if they are compensated so that they are indifferent between staying and going. Examine Figure 12.8 and decide whether the remaining partners can provide adequate compensation to persuade a partner to leave. Assume that an alternative position, paying w_1, can be found by any economist who leaves.

(a) What savings do the remaining partners make when a partner leaves? Label this point R on Figure 12.8.

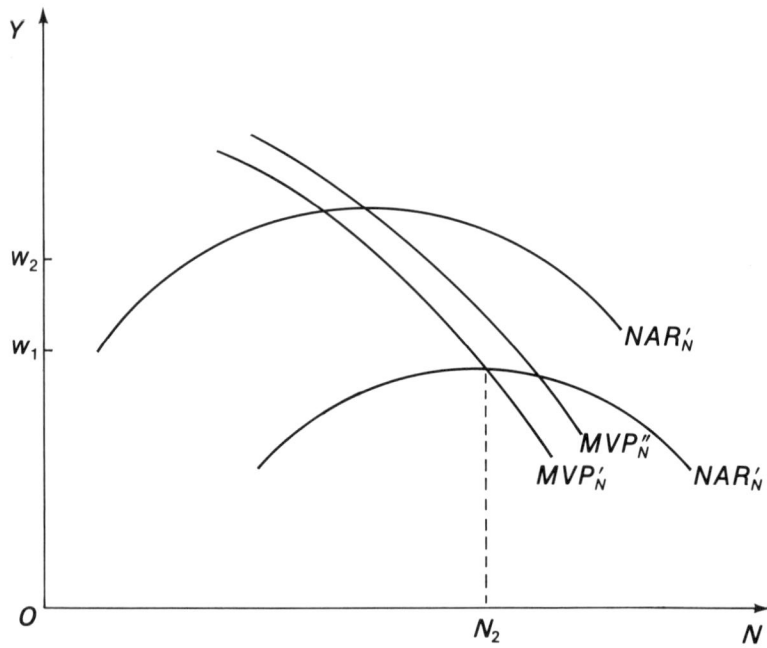

Figure 12.8

(b) While the remaining surplus would be divided up amongst fewer partners, the firm would lose this partner's contribution to output. What is this contribution? Label this point T on the diagram.

(c) What compensation would be necessary to leave a person indifferent between staying on with her current firm or moving to another firm?

(d) Will the firm's net savings be able to cover the required compensation in this case?

Question 15 What difference would it make if any partner leaving the firm were able to get another position paying w_2 instead of w_1?

Question 16 Sometimes a partner will wish to leave but the remaining partners may not wish her to go. Suppose that a firm is currently in equilibrium and one partner wishes to leave as she can earn more elsewhere.

(a) The remaining partners will not want her to leave. Why?

(b) In this case, given the rules outlined above, the partner who wishes to leave could only go if she compensates the remaining members. Can she pay sufficient compensation so that the remaining partners agree to her leaving and she still finds it advantageous to move?

Question 17 Whether or not the remaining partners will agree to a partner leaving depends on that partner's share in the surplus and her contribution to that surplus, i.e. whether her share as partner (Y) is greater or less than her contribution (MVP_N). If a partner wishes to leave and her $MVP < Y$, will the other partners agree to her going?

Although we have assumed that all partners received equal shares in the surplus, this will not always be the case. If a firm decides to expand, the existing partners could take on 'junior' partners who receive smaller shares of the surplus.

Question 18 If partners receive unequal shares, will this affect their decision to leave or stay, and the amount of compensation paid?

Our analysis has shown that in some respects partnerships operate differently from entrepreneurial firms. Before we leave this topic, consider briefly why producers may prefer to set up in partnership rather than another type of enterprise.

Question 19 Are any categories of products more often supplied by
group partnerships than by other types of firm?

From Question 1, when we asked you to consider the firm's production function, we have implicitly assumed that we could measure the firm's output. Services are, however, notoriously difficult to measure. The first order conditions that you derived in answer to Questions 8 and 9 assume that it is possible to measure the product of each individual input and, moreover, do this costlessly. Furthermore, we assumed that all economists were equally productive. Consider this last assumption: at the start of the exercise we suggested that you were about to hold a meeting to decide whether or not to take on additional partners. You now know that in order to maximise income shares you should take on sufficient partners so that the value of the marginal product of an additional economist is equal to the net average revenue generated. Now, if you all decide to recruit additional partner(s), you will only wish to admit them if you are confident that each of them is as productive as the rest of you.

Question 20 How could you establish that new recruits are as
productive as you?

Your problems will not end with establishing the productivity of any new partner; even if all partners are equally able, they may not all be equally industrious. If it is difficult to measure output, it may be very difficult to make sure that everyone pulls their weight. Monitoring the effort put in by each partner is not likely to be costless and it may not be easy to spot if anyone is shirking.

Question 21 Are the incentives to shirk likely to be the same in a
partnership as in an entrepreneurial firm and are the
monitoring costs similar?

Question 22 Can you think of any other reasons why people may set
up in partnership rather than run their own business?

If you would like to follow up theories of why different types of firm have evolved, read Coase (1937) and Alchian and Demsetz (1972). Rubin (1978) may also interest you as he examines why some firms operate franchises rather than run subsidiaries under managers.

The model we have studied in this exercise is one that underlies a large number of studies of different types of labour-managed firms. There are other variants and you might like to have a look at a utility-maximising model such as that used by Sen (1966) and Ireland and Law (1981) to analyse the labour-incentive effects of different ways of distributing the surplus. We have only studied short-run decisions and if you would like to extend your knowledge of the theory, I suggest you read Ireland and Law (1982) or Stephen (1984) who provide a detailed treatment. If your interest is more on the applied side, then Estrin (1983) tests the model against the evidence of Yugoslav self-managed firms, while Stephen (1982) combines a brief introduction to the theory with various country studies. Pauly and Redisch (1973) use the basic model we have studied to consider doctors in not-for-profit hospitals in America.

References

*Alchian, Armen A. and Demsetz, Harold (1972) 'Production, information costs, and economic organization', *American Economic Review*, 62, pp. 777—795.

Coase, R.H. (1937) 'The nature of the firm', *Economica*, New Series, 4, pp. 386—405.

Estrin, Saul (1983) *Self-Management: Economic Theory and Yugoslav Practice*, Cambridge University Press.

Ireland, N.J. and Law, P.J. (1981) 'Efficiency, incentives and individual labor supply in the labor-managed firm', *Journal of Comparative Economics*, 5, pp. 1—23.

Ireland, N.J. and Law, P.J. (1982) *The Economics of Labour-Managed Enterprises*, Croom Helm.

*Meade, J.E. (1972) 'The theory of labour-managed firms and of profit sharing', *Economic Journal*, 82, pp. 402—428.

*Pauly, Mark and Redisch, Michael (1973) 'The not-for-profit hospital as a physicians' cooperative', *American Economic Review*, 63, pp. 87—99.

Rubin, Paul H. (1978) 'The theory of the firm and the structure of the franchise contract', *Journal of Law and Economics*, 21, pp. 223—234.

Sen, Amartya K. (1966) 'Labour allocation in a cooperative enterprise', *Review of Economic Studies*, 33, pp. 361—371.

Stephen, Frank H. (ed.) (1982) *The Performance of Labour-Managed Firms*, Macmillan.

Stephen, Frank H. (1984) *The Economic Analysis of Producers' Cooperatives*, Macmillan.

---

*Suggested supplementary reading.

13

Prawns and Herring: Part I

*In this chapter we examine a fishing industry and see
how problems can arise because property rights in the
basic resource — fish — are held in common.*

*Under ideal conditions, market prices reflect what
people are prepared to pay at the margin for a good or
service as well as the marginal cost to society of producing the good. Thus, in competitive markets, prices play
an important role in informing producers of people's
preferences for different commodities and in informing
consumers of the opportunity cost of meeting their
demands. Providing certain conditions are met, such
markets result in an efficient allocation of resources —
that is to say, an allocation of resources so that it is
impossible to make one person better off except by
making another worse off. However, the ideal conditions are not always met and then the market fails to
achieve this efficient allocation. There are various
reasons why the market may fail. We have already
studied two causes of failure in earlier problems: in
Problem 4 we saw that informational asymmetries may
result in the insurance market failing and in Problem 9
we examined the effects of monopoly. Another
widespread cause of market failure is the presence of
technological externalities. If markets are to function
efficiently, property rights must be well defined.
Sometimes, however, it is not possible to assign property
rights over certain resources or enforce them if assigned.
In such cases, property rights will be held in common.*

*Ocean fishing is an example of an industry based on
common property rights. Fish are a scarce resource, but
no one person owns the fish in the sea as private property rights would be impossible to enforce. Given common ownership, fishermen will treat fish as a free
resource. At any point in time, the stock is given and
the more fish that any one fisherman catches, the fewer
fish there are left for others to catch. Each fisherman's*

catch thus depends on his own efforts and the efforts of other fishermen, and when any fisherman increases his catch, he raises the cost of catching fish for other fishermen. When the activity of one agent (individual, household or firm) affects the utility or production possibilities of another agent, without being reflected in market prices, then a technological externality exists. Fishermen consider only their private costs and benefits and ignore the external costs of their actions. Costs to society, however, include both private and external costs. For an efficient allocation of resources, we require prices to reflect marginal social benefits and to be equal to marginal social costs. The price consumers pay for fish reflects the fishermen's private costs which are less than the marginal social costs of the fishery.

In the first part of this two-part problem we analyse how common property rights result in too much effort going into fishing. One consequence of this is that over time the fish stock may be depleted or even destroyed and we examine how the conditions for an optimal catch rate are determined. In the next chapter we discuss possible policies that could be adopted in order to manage a fishery to ensure that this catch rate is not exceeded.

Before you start the problem check your understanding of the following:

(a) determination of market equilibrium where entry is unrestricted;
(b) property rights;
(c) the conditions for a Pareto-efficient allocation of resources;
(d) Pareto efficiency and competitive markets;
(e) the distinction between pecuniary and technological externalities.

The Sunday Times Magazine, 15 January 1978, published an article about Hugh Allen who, five years earlier, quit his job in the Personnel Department of Lucas in Birmingham to become a prawn fisherman in the Western Isles.

Prawns are found in mud at depths between 200 and 1200 feet. They are caught by creels which are cages with holes in them through which the prawns pass for the bait. Sixty or seventy creels are made up into a 'fleet'. These fleets are buoyed at each end and dropped onto the prawn grounds and raised after a day. Each fleet can yield several stone of prawns and Allen normally fished twelve fleets a day. The price for prawns at that time was £12 a stone — almost £1 a pound — which was why, at 1978 prices, *The Sunday Times* called Allen 'highly successful'.

Using creels, the prawns are taken whole and alive. A trawl net would damage and kill them; nevertheless Allen was thinking of trawling for prawns. The net is dragged between two boats and, although it damages the catch, far more are caught. Allen would need a more powerful boat to trawl and this would mean a large capital outlay. After considering the running costs, he reckoned he could clear at least £15,000 a year.

The problems we examine in this exercise are:

(i) why a fishery, to which there is open access, may not be fished in an optimal fashion (Part I);

(ii) how such a fishery could be managed so that the fish stock is not damaged or destroyed (Part II).

We start by noting that prawns are what we call a 'common property' resource: no single person owns them, so prawns are free goods.

Question 1 Can you give other examples of common property resources?

Question 2 Are common property resources always both free and scarce?

Question 3 What is the difference between a natural resource and a common property resource?

Some resources are exhaustible. A resource is defined as exhaustible 'if it is possible to find a pattern of use which makes its supply dwindle to zero' (Dasgupta and Heal 1979, p. 3).

Question 4 Prawns, and more generally fish, can and do reproduce themselves. Does this mean that they are not an 'exhaustible resource'? Explain your answer.

Question 5 When the *Sunday Times Magazine* article was written, Allen was the only prawn fisher in the Western Isles. Do you think that the 'pattern of use' he had established would result in overfishing of prawns?

Question 6 Do you think that it is likely that Allen is still the only person fishing for prawns in the area?

Question 7 What difference would it make if other people were to set up as prawn fishers in the same area as Allen? How would this affect his catch rate and his profits?

In order to understand what happens when there is open access to a fishery, we will study what has happened to the herring fishery over the past thirty years. The *Encyclopaedia Britannica* states that the herring is 'probably the most abundant fish in the near surface waters of the seas' (1982, Micropaedia, p. 9), yet in 1977 a ban was imposed on fishing for herring in the North Sea for fear that stocks would be completely destroyed through overfishing. While we hope that this is an exceptional case (but think of whales!), it is nevertheless worth studying how herring stocks came to be so depleted, for if such things can happen where stocks are huge, it might also occur with other types of fish.

First of all, a little background information. North Sea herring eat plankton and live in vast schools. There are various distinct groups and they spawn in different seasons and on different grounds. For example, Buchan

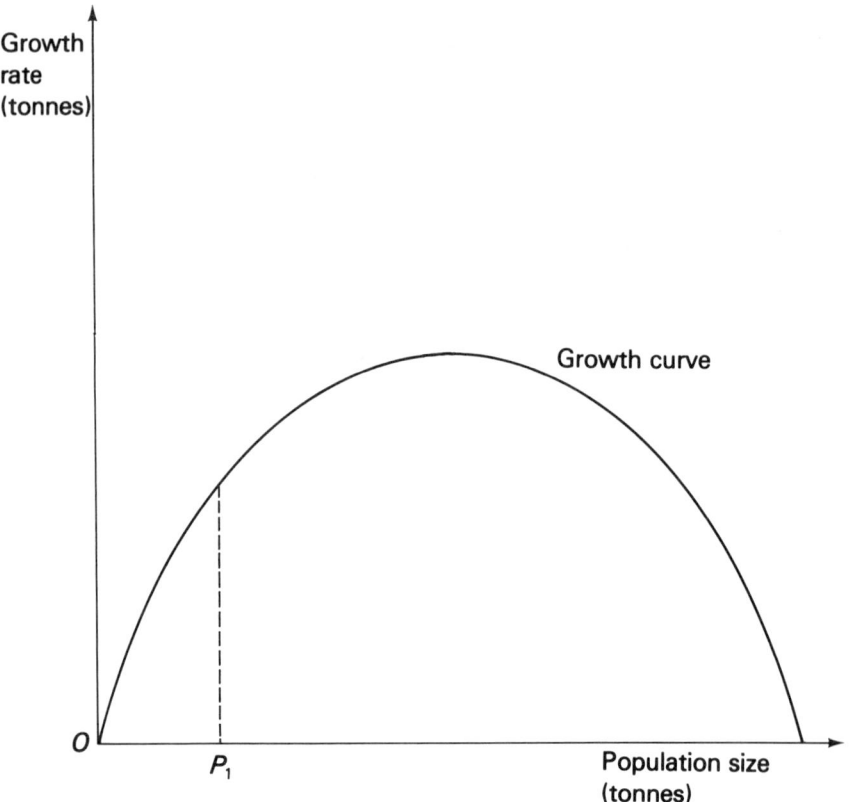

Figure 13.1

herring spawn near Scotland in August and September and then migrate to Norway; Downs herring spawn in November to January off the French coast and feed all summer in the North Sea. Herring do not breed at a given age but when they reach a certain size. The more plentiful their food is, the faster they grow and the earlier they breed. Moreover, the larger they are, the more eggs they lay. The *Encyclopaedia Britannica* reports that around 1925 most herring bred at the age of five years, but in 1950—52 they bred when four years old and from 1952 at three years. The reason for this was a more abundant supply of their main food (1982, Macropaedia Vol. 14, p. 829).

The herring population will grow as long as reproduction exceeds mortality. While herring may live for twenty years, most are likely to die much younger, a death rate of 72 per cent in their eleventh year being usual. Mortality depends on the number of predators (other than man) and natural causes. If we measure the herring population by weight, then weight in any year will depend on the reproduction rate, the growth rate of each herring (one tonne of herring can be made up of lots of little herring or fewer large ones) and natural mortality. Biological studies suggest that the growth curve for a fishery will be bell-shaped as in Figure 13.1.

When the population is small, say P_1, reproduction and individual growth rates will exceed mortality rates and there will be a net increase in population. However, as the population size rises, the growth rate will begin to decline and eventually reproduction and individual growth are exactly offset by mortality so that the population ceases to grow and is in equilibrium.

Question 8   On Figure 13.1 show:

(a) the population size at which the growth rate is at its highest;

(b) the natural equilibrium population size (label this P^*).

If man did not fish for herring, the population stock would remain at P^* (unless ecological conditions changed). However, when man joins the natural predators, a new equilibrium will be established where the increase from reproduction and individual growth is balanced by the decrease due to natural factors and man's catch.[1]

---

1. Any new equilibrium will also be affected by the catch rate for any of the herring's natural predators, e.g. cod, mackerel, tuna and sharks. Moreover, if other fishes share the same food supply, the catch rate of these fishes will also affect the herring growth rate. The increase in food supply in the early 1950s was probably due to catches of other fishes. We ignore such interdependencies here, although where they exist they complicate considerably the matter of fishery management (as we shall see later).

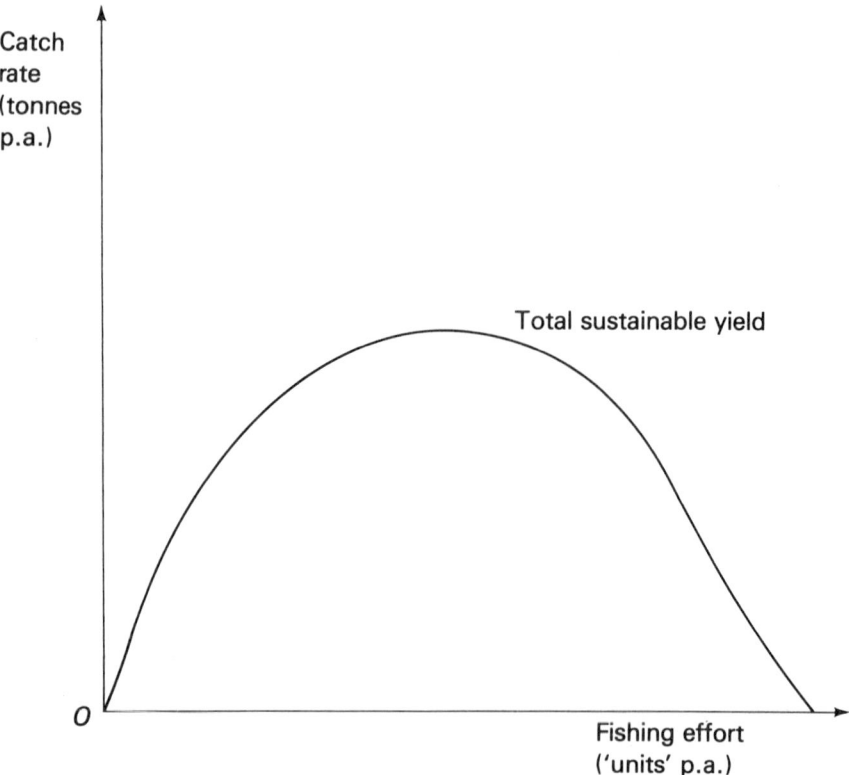

Figure 13.2

The herring industry's catch rate will thus depend on the population stock as well as the amount of effort it puts into fishing. We assume that we can measure fishing effort by inputs such as the number of vessels, nets and time spent fishing, so that with a given technique (e.g. drift nets), a fixed number of boats and amount of time, we can talk of a unit of fishing effort. Increasing the number of boats and other inputs increases the level of effort. To simplify the analysis at this stage we assume that all fishermen are equally skilful at catching fish. This assumption will be relaxed later.

As the catch depends on both the level of fishing effort and the population stock, we now need to find the catch rate which can be sustained at each level of effort so that the herring stock is not damaged or destroyed. The fish population is in equilibrium where the catch rate equals the growth rate; providing the catch rate does not exceed the growth rate there is no danger of damaging the stock. We must therefore calculate the population equilibrium rate *for each level of effort* and in this way derive the 'total sustainable yield curve' which shows the sustainable catch rate of herring plotted for different levels of effort. This curve is, in effect, the herring industry's long-run production function, and such a curve is drawn in Figure 13.2.

Question 9   What is the maximum sustainable yield that can be achieved? Mark this *MSY* on Figure 13.2.

Question 10 Over what range of effort is there over-fishing of herring?

It has been estimated that the maximum sustainable yield for North Sea herring is between 700,000 and 800,000 tonnes per annum. In the early 1950s the average catch rate was about 600,000 tonnes p.a., but from the late 1950s more and more fishermen turned from drift nets to purse seine nets and acoustic fish detectors, raising catch rates per vessel (Wise, 1984, pp. 60—62).

Question 11 What effect would this technological change have had on the total sustainable yield curve? Draw in the new curve on Figure 13.2.

About the same time, Danish and Norwegian fleets increased their catches in order to supply fishmeal and fish oil factories. North Sea herring landings peaked in 1965 at around 1,200,000 tonnes and after this fell steeply, so that by 1975 landings were less than 300,000 tonnes p.a. In 1977 a total ban was placed on herring fishing in the North Sea which was lifted only in the summer of 1983 (Wise, loc. cit.).

Why did fishermen continue to fish for herring when it must have been clear that they were in danger of destroying their livelihood? The answer lies in the fact that they held common property rights in herring. People will continue to fish as long as the revenue they derive from fishing exceeds their costs and, as long as there are above normal profits to be earned, additional boats will enter the industry. With each additional boat the average catch rate for the fishery will fall — but this is not something that will deter the individual boat-owner as long as he is earning sufficient revenue from his catch to cover his costs. Because fishermen hold common rights in the stock of fish, a stock externality exists: each fisherman's catch depends not only on his own efforts but also on the efforts of other fishermen and their numbers. As Clark points out, common property rights in the fishing stock result in fishermen being faced with the prisoner's dilemma: they will all gain if they co-operate but each individual has an incentive not to co-operate (Clark 1982, p. 286).

Our next step in the analysis is therefore to consider the fishery's costs. Total costs in this case depend not only on expenditure on capital and labour but also on the sustainable yields. In order to plot the total cost curve of the

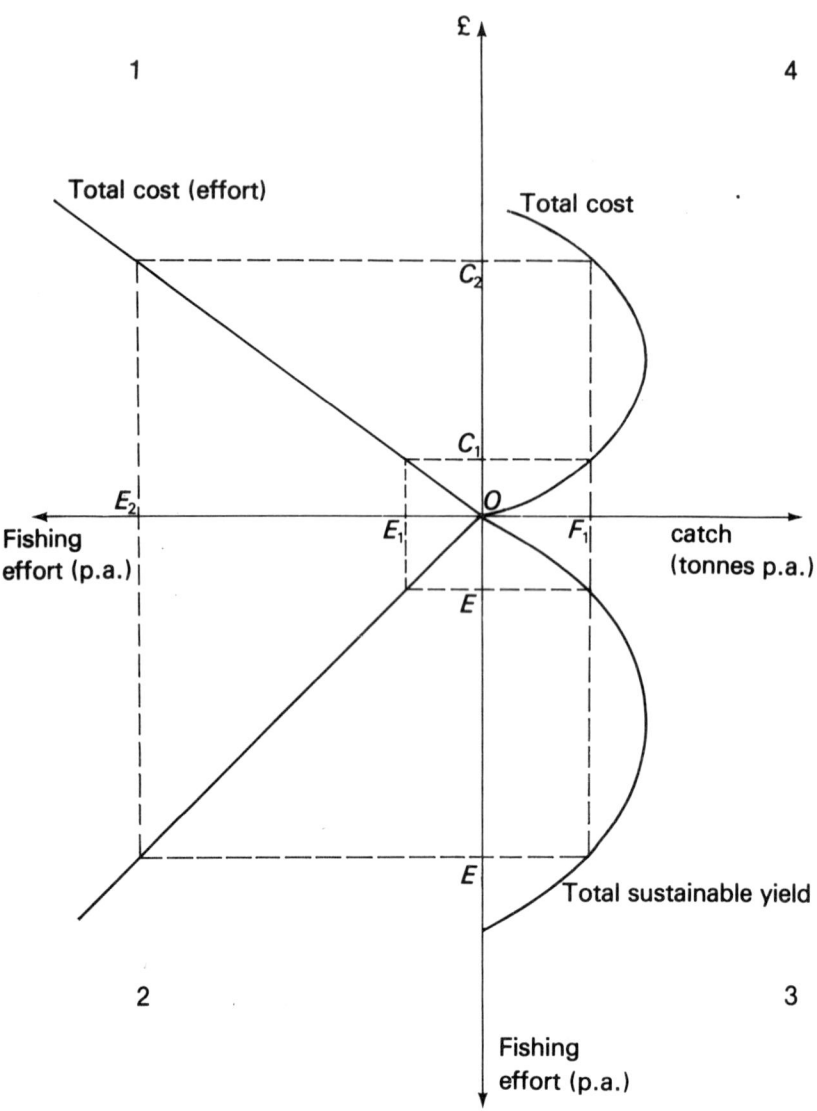

Figure 13.3

herring fishery we use the quadrant diagram in Figure 13.3. This may look a bit complicated, but it is quite easy to understand if you interpret it quadrant by quadrant.

Quadrant 1 shows the total cost of *effort*; as we have drawn it here, this rises at a constant rate as effort increases because we have assumed that all fishermen are equally skilful at catching fish. Quadrant 3 shows the total sustainable yield curve we examined in Figure 13.2 and Quadrant 2 is a link diagram between Quadrants 1 and 3. Using these three quadrants, we can plot the total cost curve in Quadrant 4.

We start in Quadrant 1: if fishing effort is at level E_1, we use the link diagram to move to Quadrant 3 where we find the catch rate that can be sustained at this level of effort, i.e. F_1. Returning to Quadrant 1, we see that the total cost of effort level F_1 is C_1 (measured on the vertical axis) and we can thus plot the point (C_1, F_1) in Quadrant 4. This represents the total cost of F_1 tonnes of herring. If you repeat this for different levels of effort, the total cost curve can be plotted.

Question 12 At effort level, E_2, the sustainable yield is F_1, i.e. the same as at effort level E_1, but the cost is C_2. Why is this?

Question 13 At what catch level does the total cost turn backwards?

Question 14 The next step is to derive the average and marginal cost curves. How can you derive them from the total cost curve in Quadrant 4?

If we had information about total effort (in terms of boats, etc.) together with data on costs of operating and maintaining the vessels, on wages, etc., we could derive the cost curves for the herring fishery as Bell (1972) has done for the New England lobster fishery. Unfortunately we do not have this data and thus the average and marginal cost curves drawn in Figure 13.4 are not based on empirical estimates and the (imaginary) figures are shown for illustration only. *They do not represent actual costs and prices for the fishery.*

The optimal catch rate for the herring fishery is where the marginal cost of an additional tonne of herring is equal to the price that people are willing to pay for it.

Question 15 Suppose that demand for North Sea herring is given by D_1 in Figure 13.4:

(a) Find the fishery's optimal catch.
(b) What is the profit made by the fishery, if any, at this catch rate?

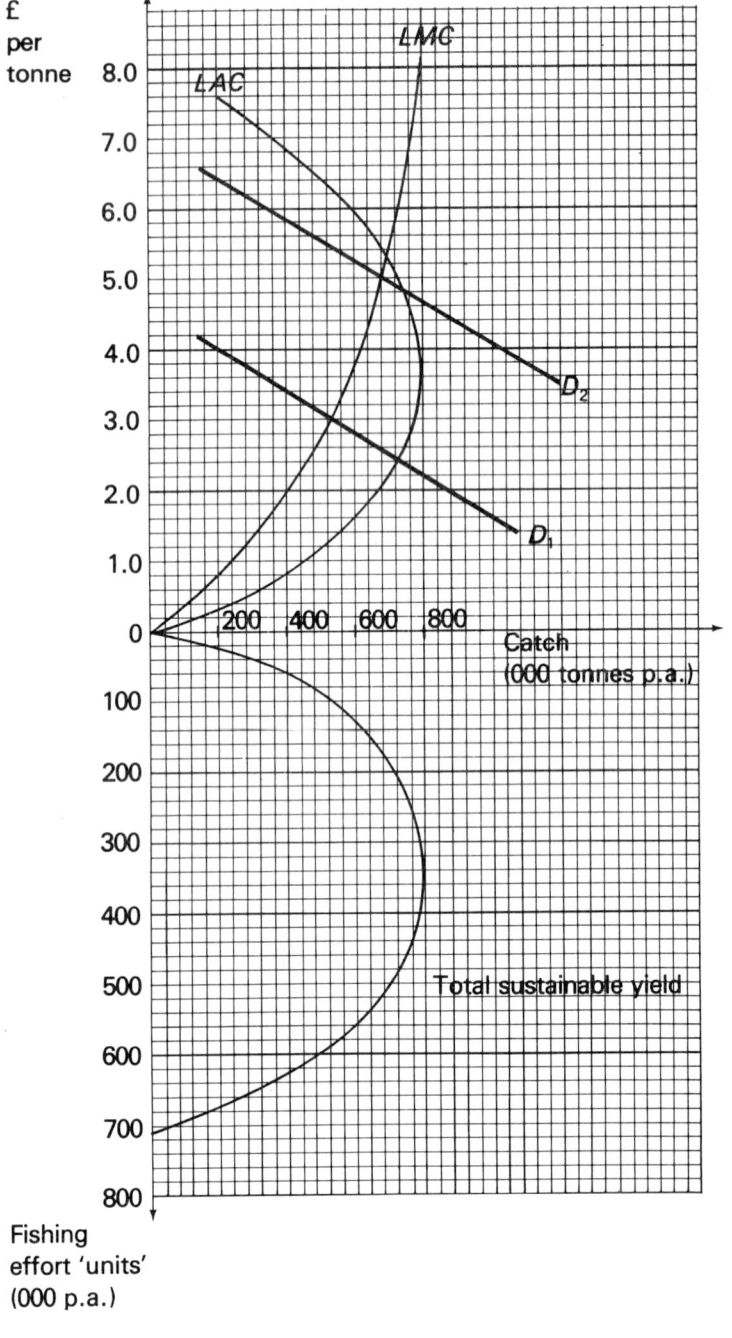

Figure 13.4

Question 16 Is this catch rate the equilibrium catch rate for the fishery? Explain your answer carefully.

Question 17 Now suppose that demand for herring rises from D_1 to D_2. What is the equilibrium output of the fishery now?

Question 18 Comparing catch rates at different demand levels:

    (a) By what proportion has the level of fishing effort risen at (i) the equilibrium and (ii) the optimal levels, when demand shifts from D_1 to D_2?

    (b) By what proportion has the catch rate risen at (i) the equilibrium and (ii) the optimal levels?

Question 19 Is the long-run average cost curve the supply curve for the herring fishery?

Question 20 In your own words, explain why the optimal catch rate will be exceeded by a fishery with unrestricted entry and contrast the fishery with a perfectly competitive industry based on a renewable resource.

Question 21 We started this exercise by considering Hugh Allen who was fishing for prawns in the Western Isles. Suppose that a fishery is fished by one fisherman or, alternatively, by one company which has a monopoly. Will the optimal catch be exceeded in these cases?

Our analysis has shown that in a fishery with open access, economic rents will be dissipated and the optimal catch rate exceeded. If you are interested in learning more about the economics of fisheries, I would suggest that you read Anderson (1977) who provides a detailed analysis. The derivation of the long-run cost curves of the fishery can also be found in Copes (1970), while an interesting empirical study is that of Bell (1972) who has estimated the production function and cost curves for the US northern lobster fishery.

The problems of managing an open access fishery are complex even if that fishery is confined to one country. The migratory habits of the North Sea herring and the location of the spawning and feeding grounds within easy reach of many countries has meant that fishermen of various nationalities make up the herring fishery. It is hardly surprising, therefore, that negotiation of fishing rights between the European Community and other interested countries has been so protracted and difficult. If you are interested in the fisheries policy of the Common Market, you will find a comprehensive account of it and its evolution in Wise (op. cit.).

In the second part of this exercise we examine the proposals that have been put forward for the regulation of fisheries in order to achieve the optimal catch rate.

References

Anderson, Lee G. (1977) *The Economics of Fisheries Management*, John Hopkins University Press.

*Bell, Frederick W. (1972) 'Technological externalities and common-property resources: an empirical study of the US northern lobster fishery', *Journal of Political Economy*, 80, pp. 148—153.

Clark, Colin W. (1982) 'Models of fishery regulation', in Leonard J. Mirman and Daniel F. Spulber (eds), *Essays on the Economics of Renewable Resources*, North Holland Publishing Company.

*Copes, Parzival (1970) 'The backward-bending supply curve of the fishing industry', *Scottish Journal of Political Economy*, 17, pp. 69—77.

Dasgupta, P.S. and Heal, G.M. (1979) *Economic Theory and Exhaustible Resources*, Cambridge University Press.

Encyclopaedia Britannica (1982), Micro- and Macropaedia.

Wise, Mark (1984) *The Common Fisheries Policy of the European Community*, Methuen.

---

*Suggested supplementary reading.

14

Prawns and Herring: Part II

In the second part of our analysis of the herring fishery, we examine how the industry might be managed to prevent over-fishing. Where there are many fishermen involved, it is unlikely that they can reach agreement amongst themselves to ensure that the optimal catch rate is not exceeded and it seems probable that the government (or governments) will have to intervene.

Various forms of regulation are possible. Here we consider three options: licensing, quotas and taxation. Our main concern will be with their effectiveness in achieving and maintaining the optimal catch rate. However, we must not neglect other important considerations such as the political and administrative feasibility of different forms of regulation. Moreover, any evaluation of intervention to eliminate the welfare loss arising from market failure must also consider the costs of collective action. If such costs exceed any gain from eliminating the welfare loss, then intervention will not be appropriate.

The analysis undertaken in this problem builds on that of Problem 13; the only difference is that we now discuss the determination of an efficient resource allocation within the herring fishery in terms of effort rather than catch rate. If you have coped with the earlier problems in this book, you should have no difficulty in tackling this final problem.

We have seen in Part I that when there is open access to a fishery, too much effort may go into catching fish. This is undesirable for two reasons: it can result in over-fishing and the catch may be obtained at excessive cost.

There are so many fishermen of different nationalities who fish for herring in the North Sea that there is no possibility that the optimal level of catch can be achieved by the herring fishery regulating its own catch rate and, therefore, some outside body, probably the governments, must introduce regulation. As we noted in Part I, the European Community and Norway did ban fishing for herring in the North Sea for some years and have now agreed a common fisheries policy. In this exercise we shall concentrate on analysing alternative methods of regulation so as to understand their relative merits and weaknesses and, in order to avoid the complications of international politics, we discuss these in relation to the fishery and ignore the fact that various countries are involved. It will not be difficult for you to assess the additional problems that arise when fishermen from more than one nation make up a fishery.

In Part I we analysed the problem of open access fisheries by concentrating on the industry as a whole and did not consider in any detail the firm, which we shall take to be the individual boat. We now need to extend our analysis to understand the effect of regulation on both the boat and the fishery. The problem faced by any regulatory agency is how to reduce the level of effort put into fishing so that the optimal catch rate is not exceeded. It is not sufficient to specify an optimal catch rate: the optimal levels of effort at boat and fishery level have to be considered so that the catch is not taken by inefficient use of resources. We start our analysis by examining the factors that affect the level of effort expended on fishing and we draw on Anderson's work (1977, particularly Chapter 3).

We assume that fishermen aim to maximise profits and that they catch only one species of fish, herring. For the moment we shall continue to assume that all fishermen are equally skilled, so that we can talk of a representative

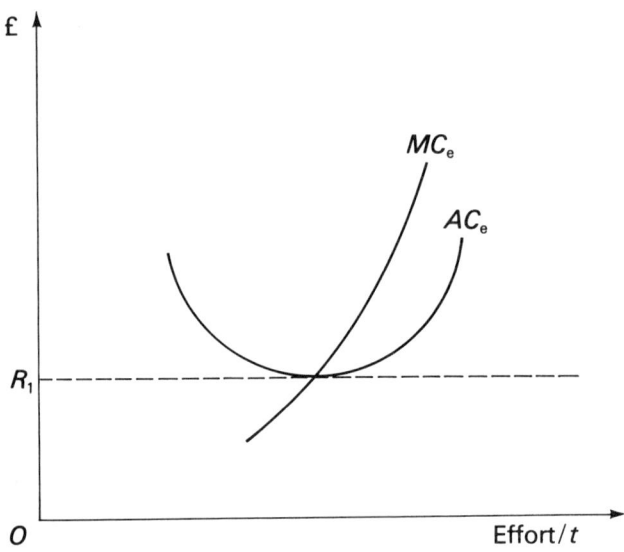

Figure 14.1

boat, and we assume that individual boats face the same costs. You will remember that we measured the industry fishing effort by inputs such as boats, nets, equipment and time spent fishing and, given our assumption that all individual boats face the same costs, the total cost of effort for the fishery rises at a constant rate. In other words, any new boat that enters the fishery is similar to other boats and has an equally skilled crew. This means that for the industry, the long-run average cost curve for effort is constant and, therefore, equal to the long-run marginal cost of effort.

We now need to consider the cost curves for the individual boat. The input of capital in the form of the boat, gear, nets, etc., is fixed, and as effort in the form of labour increases, average fixed costs will fall. Eventually, however, the average cost of effort will start to rise (why?) and thus the individual boat will face U-shaped average cost curves for effort, as shown in Figure 14.1. (Note that we shall use a small e to represent effort by the individual boat and a large E for fishery effort.)

The individual boat's catch is small in relation to the total fishery catch, and return for each unit of effort expended in any period of time is given by the boat's average catch per unit of *effort* multiplied by the price of herring.

Question 1 Suppose that the representative boat is currently receiving a return equal to R_1 per unit of effort, as shown in Figure 14.1. How much effort will go into fishing? Is a profit being made?

Question 2 What would happen if the return were to rise?

Question 3 What is the *individual boat's* supply curve of effort? How do we find the *fishery's* short-run supply curve of effort? What will this curve look like?

We now need to find the average and marginal revenue of effort schedules for the fishery to show how the return to effort is determined for the fishery as a whole. We start by returning to the total sustainable yield curve we studied in Part I. You will remember this shows the catch rates that can be sustained at each level of fishery effort. In order to simplify our analysis we assume that the fishery faces a given price for herring.[1] With this assumption it is simple to plot the fishery's total revenue schedule: for each level of effort we can find the sustainable yield and multiplying this by the given price, we

---

1. The assumption of a given price is not realistic for the herring fishery and does not accord with the downward-sloping demand curve we drew in Part I. However, when the price varies, if the maximum sustainable yield is greater than the catch rate which yields the maximum revenue for any given demand curve, the total revenue schedule will have two maxima. By taking the price as given, we avoid the problem of multiple equilibria (see Anderson, op. cit.).

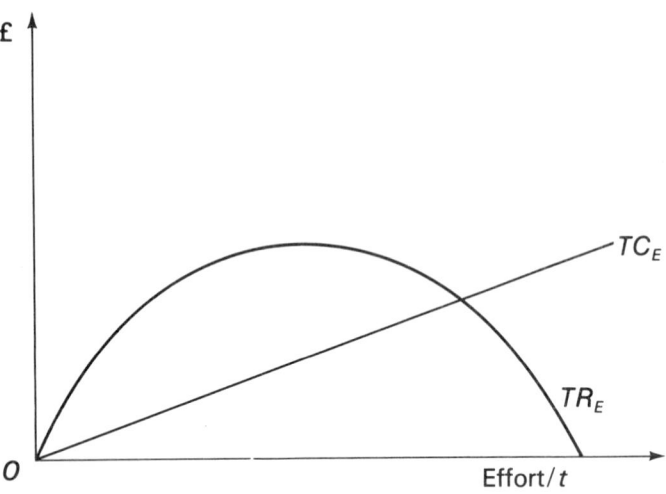

Figure 14.2

obtain the total revenue. The total revenue schedule (TR_E) is shown on Figure 14.2 together with the total cost of effort schedule (TC_E) for the fishery.

We can now plot the relevant average and marginal schedules from the total revenue and total cost schedules in Figure 14.2. The average return per unit of effort for the fishery is equal to the average catch multiplied by price $(PF/E$, where F is the catch rate), while the marginal return is the change in the catch rate as effort is increased, again multiplied by price $(P\Delta F/\Delta E)$. Both of these fall as effort increases, as can be seen in Figure 14.3.

As we have already noted, the long-run marginal cost of effort for the fishery is constant. The short-run supply of effort schedule is the sum of the marginal cost of effort curves for individual boats making up the fishery (see Question 3) and we have drawn in such a short-run schedule, ΣMC_1, in Figure 14.3.

We can now see that when the short-run supply of effort is ΣMC_1, the rate of return to the fishery will be R_2, and the total effort supplied is E_2. Figure 14.3 has been redrawn as Figure 14.4(b) alongside the diagram for a representative boat, Figure 14.4(a).

Question 4   What level of effort will the individual boat supply when the rate of return in the fishery equals R_2?

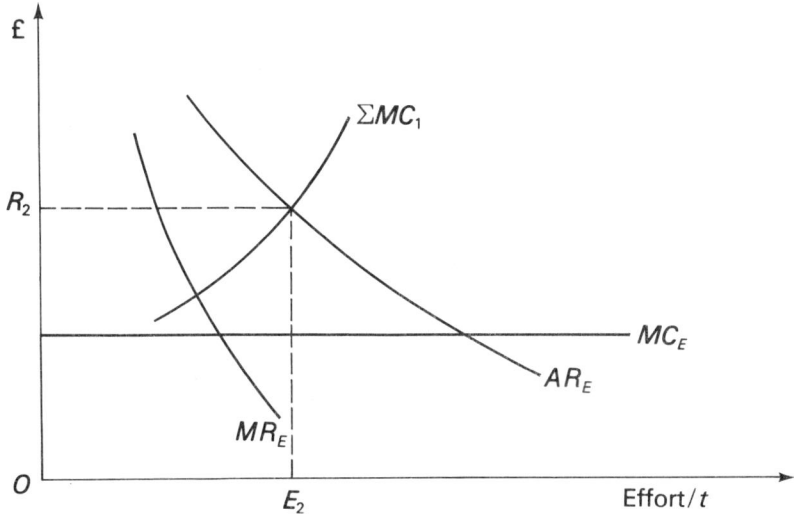

Figure 14.3

Question 5   (a) At what rate of return will the fishery be in long-
                     run equilibrium?
                (b) When the fishery is in equilibrium, what is the
                     level of effort supplied by the individual boat?

With open access, as long as supra-normal profits can be made, additional
boats will enter the fishery and, given our assumption of equal skills,
equilibrium will occur where the fishery's long-run marginal cost curve cuts
the average revenue schedule. As additional boats have entered the fishery,
the short-run supply curve of effort has shifted outwards and the long-run
equilibrium thus represents an excessive application of effort. The optimal
level is where the long-run marginal cost of effort is equal to the marginal
revenue from effort, i.e. at E^* in Figure 14.5(b). At the boat level, the
optimal amount of effort is e^*. However, as can be seen from Figure 14.5(a),
at fishery effort level E^* the rate of return is R^* and boats will wish to supply
a greater amount of effort than e^*.

Question 6   (a) Why is e^* the optimal level of effort by the
                     individual boat?
                (b) At e^* how much profit is a boat making? Show
                     this on Figure 14.5(a). Is this the profit-maximising
                     level of effort for the boat?

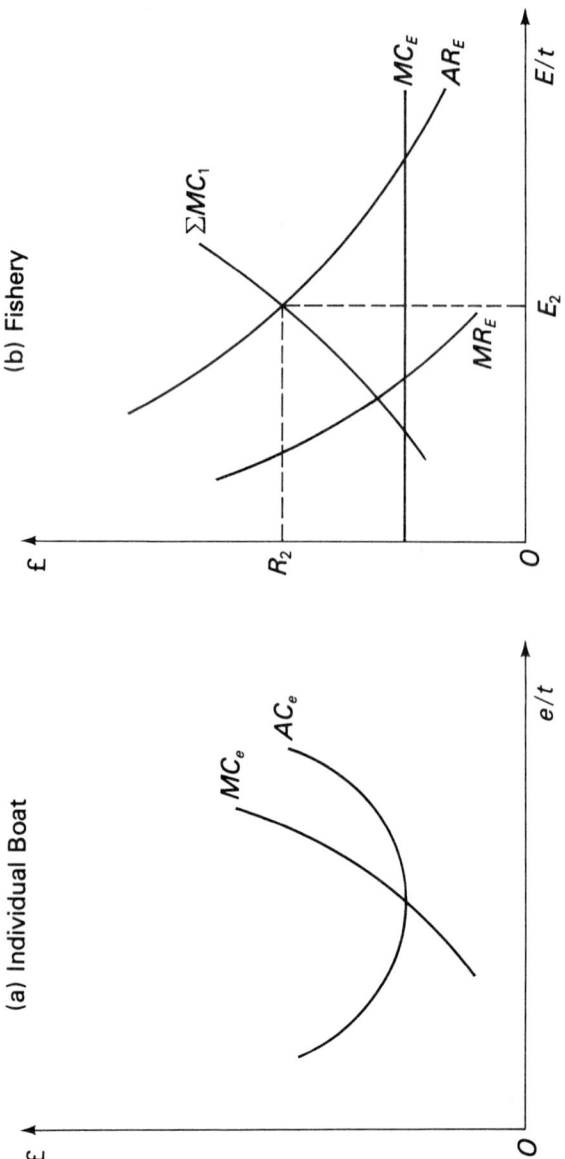

Figure 14.4

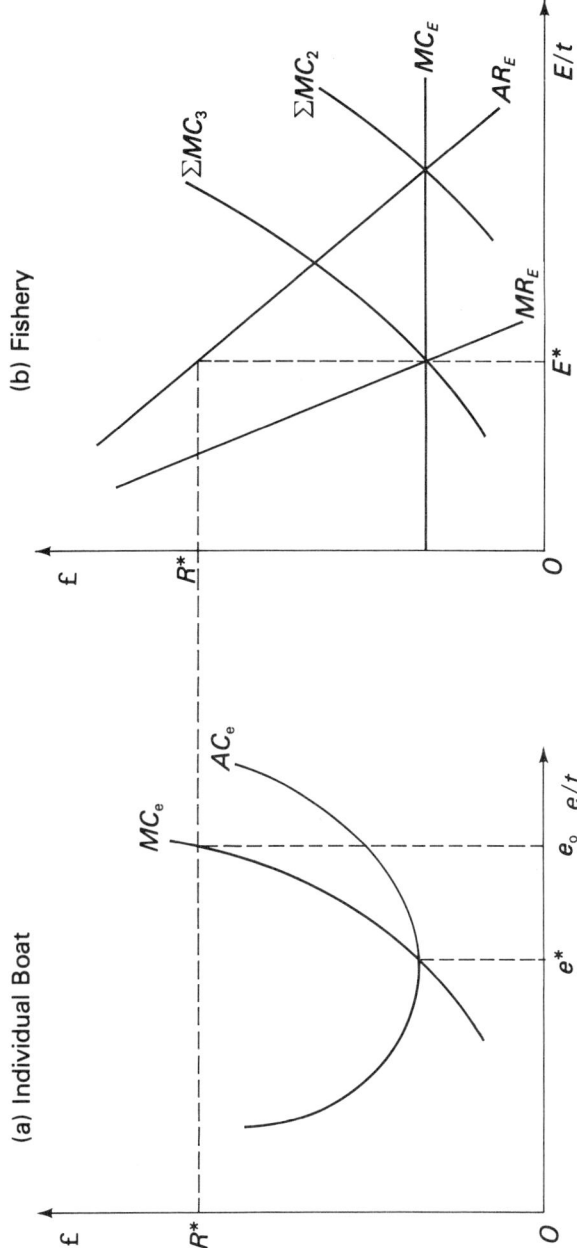

Figure 14.5

The problem facing any regulatory agency is thus twofold: it will be necessary to control the number of boats in a fishery by preventing entry if fishery effort is to be kept at level E^*; however, this policy will not achieve the optimal catch rate unless individual boats can be persuaded to operate at level e^*.

Question 7   Suppose that the regulatory agency manages to restrict the number of boats in the fishery so that the short-run supply schedule is ΣMC_3, as shown in Figure 14.5(b), but cannot ensure that boats keep to the optimal individual effort level of e^*. What will be the resulting level of effort within the *fishery* and the consequent rate of return?

The important point to understand is that it is not sufficient to restrict the number of boats in a fishery; somehow the effort of individual boats must also be restrained to achieve the optimal level of effort and hence ensure an optimal catch at minimum cost (see Anderson, op. cit., pp. 57–65).

Question 8   In Figure 14.6(b) we show a case where the fishery short-run supply curve is ΣMC_4.
(a) Does this represent an optimal allocation of effort?
(b) If so, explain why. If not, would achievement of the optimal level imply an increase or decrease in the number of boats?
(c) In Figure 14.6(a) alongside, draw in the relevant cost curves for a representative boat to illustrate your answer.

Crews of Unequal Skill

So far we have assumed that all boats had crews of equal skill and thus we were able to draw the cost curves for a representative boat. This assumption is, however, patently unrealistic and catch rates will vary between boats because of different fishing skills, levels of experience, and differences in equipment (see Copes (1972) for the discussion of why skills may vary).

When this is the case, then it means that the fishery total cost of effort curve will now rise at an increasing rate and thus the long-run marginal cost curve will be upward sloping for the fishery. One consequence of this is that not all rents will be dissipated in equilibrium: the long-run equilibrium will occur where the costs of the *marginal* boat are equal to its average return to effort, i.e. where the long-run marginal cost of effort curve cuts the average return to effort for the industry. The marginal boat will only make normal profits, but more skilled crews will still derive economic rents.

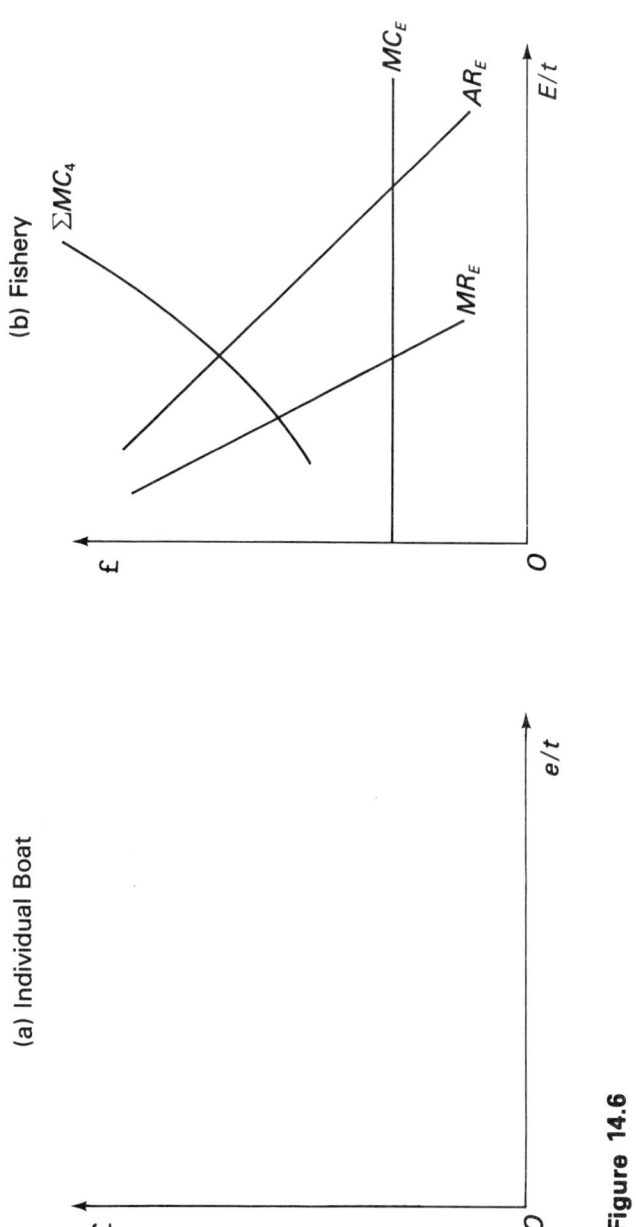

(a) Individual Boat

(b) Fishery

Figure 14.6

Question 9 Draw diagrams (using Figure 14.7) to illustrate the
optimal level of effort for a fishery where skills vary,
and relate this to diagrams representing (a) the marginal
boat in the fishery and (b) a boat with a more skilled
crew (see Figure 14.8).

Regulation

At last we can consider the options open to any regulatory agency. However,
before we examine these in detail we should consider what criteria to apply
in evaluating the various possibilities.

Our discussion has focused on the efficiency aspect of regulation, and any
instrument adopted should be judged on its ability to ensure that over-fishing
is prevented, that the catch is obtained at minimum cost and that it should
not inhibit the introduction of innovation in the form of improved fishing
techniques. However, as we have noted, regulation may well affect the
income of fishermen, particularly if it takes the form of reducing the number
of boats. Many fishing communities have few alternative employment
opportunities and any regulatory agency would therefore have to consider
the effects of any form of regulation on employment and the distribution of
income. Moreover, conditions in a fishery are rarely static and one might
expect demand for fish to change over time, or the food supply of herring
might vary, affecting the sustainable yield curve. Such changes would cause
the optimal catch rate to alter, and any regulation should be flexible enough
to be able to cope with changes in both economic and biological conditions.
One would also wish to keep administrative and monitoring costs as low as
possible.

Question 10 List possible criteria which you think should be adopted
in evaluating alternative forms of regulation.

A regulatory body has various options open to it: for example, it could
restrict the number of boats by issuing licences and prohibiting fishing
without a licence. Alternatively, it could set a quota on the total catch of
herring or it could set individual quotas at boat level. An indirect method of
regulation would be to put a tax on each tonne of herring landed; this would
reduce the return to fishermen who would thus cut back on the amount of
effort they put into fishing.

Question 11 Can you think of any other forms of regulation?

We shall concentrate on analysing the effects of licences, quotas and taxes
because between them they raise most of the issues that need to be considered.
You can extend your analysis to other forms of regulation if you wish.

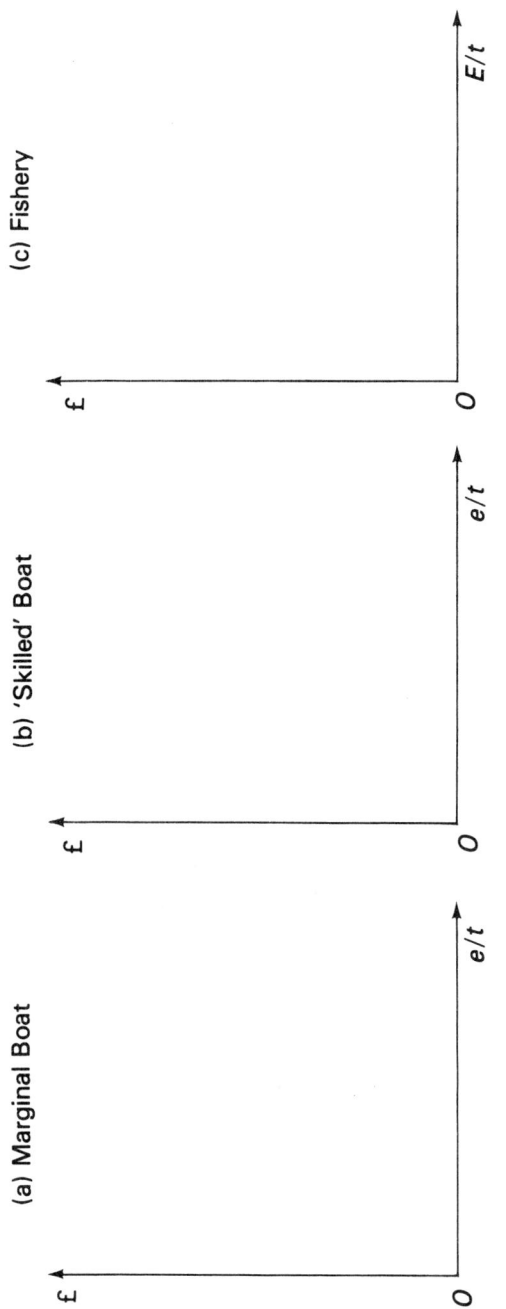

Figure 14.7

(i) Licences

As we have seen, too much effort goes into catching fish. By issuing a limited number of licences, it would be possible to restrict effort at the fishery level. However, if the number of licences issued is less than the current number of fishermen, it is necessary to consider who should receive a licence and whether compensation should be paid to those who are unlucky (and if so, how much and by whom). If an industry is currently over-fishing, it is clearly not desirable to issue all existing fishermen with licences. However, those fishermen who get the licences are being given valuable property rights and a system could develop, similar to that in the taxi market, where licence holders could sell the licence if they wished to quit the fishery (see Problem 9). One way round this might be for the licensing authority to put the licences up for auction: anyone could bid but, in this case, the money would be paid to the licensing authority and could be used to compensate unsuccessful bidders who could no longer continue to fish.

Question 12 What would determine the number of licences an agency might put up for auction?

Question 13 What would determine the price of licences?

Question 14 Would all fishermen be prepared to pay the same price for a licence?

If such a scheme were adopted, the authority would need to consider carefully the period for which such a licence would be valid. If the period is too short, this would inhibit investment, while if it is too long, new entrants might have to wait some years before getting a chance to bid. Moreover, if the underlying economic or biological conditions were to change, there would be difficulties in adjusting the catch level. One way round such problems might be to arrange the auctions so that only a certain number of licences were put up every year but each licence would be valid for a period of several years.

Question 15 Would this be a satisfactory solution or can you see any problems?

Question 16 Would such a system enable the fishery to be managed so that the optimal catch rate is not exceeded? Consider effects at the level of the individual boat as well as the fishery.

(ii) Quotas

If a quota is set for the total catch of a fishery and no restriction is made concerning the number of vessels, the overall catch rate may be optimal but it is unlikely to be achieved at minimum cost. There will be a rush at the beginning of any new quota season as vessels seek to catch herring while stocks are abundant and before the overall limit is met. As long as profits can be made, additional boats will enter. This will effectively shorten the fishing season and once the total quota has been reached, vessels will be idle unless there are alternative species they can catch, or alternative areas where they can fish. If it seems likely that such excess capacity will develop, individual quotas would seem preferable, but the problem here is how to allocate such quotas and, once allocated, how to enforce them.

Question 17 How do you think quotas should be allocated: in line with past catches, on an equal basis . . .?

Question 18 Should boats be allowed to transfer quotas?

Question 19 Should quotas be auctioned, as in the case of licences?

Consider carefully what difference it makes if you drop the assumption that all crews are equally skilful.

(iii) Taxes

As we have seen, due to the stock externalities that arise in fisheries, the catch rate of an individual boat depends not only on its own efforts but also on the efforts and number of other boats. A tax on effort would force individual boats to internalise the effects of increasing effort and thus lead each boat to adopt the optimal level of effort. However, it is difficult to devise and enforce a tax on effort, especially where skills vary, and an alternative is to tax the output. If a tax is levied on each tonne of herring landed, it would lower the average rate of return to effort and thus effectively shift the average return to effort schedule downwards to AR'_E, as shown in Figure 14.8. The optimal tax is one that equates the net average return to effort with the long-run marginal cost of effort. If we assume that all boats are equally skilled, as shown by the constant long-run marginal cost curve drawn in Figure 14.8, each individual boat now receives a net return of R_0, rather than R_1, and is thus operating at minimum average cost. There is no inducement for other boats to enter the fishery as only normal profits are being made.

Question 20 Will a tax on output result in the optimal level of effort at the boat level?

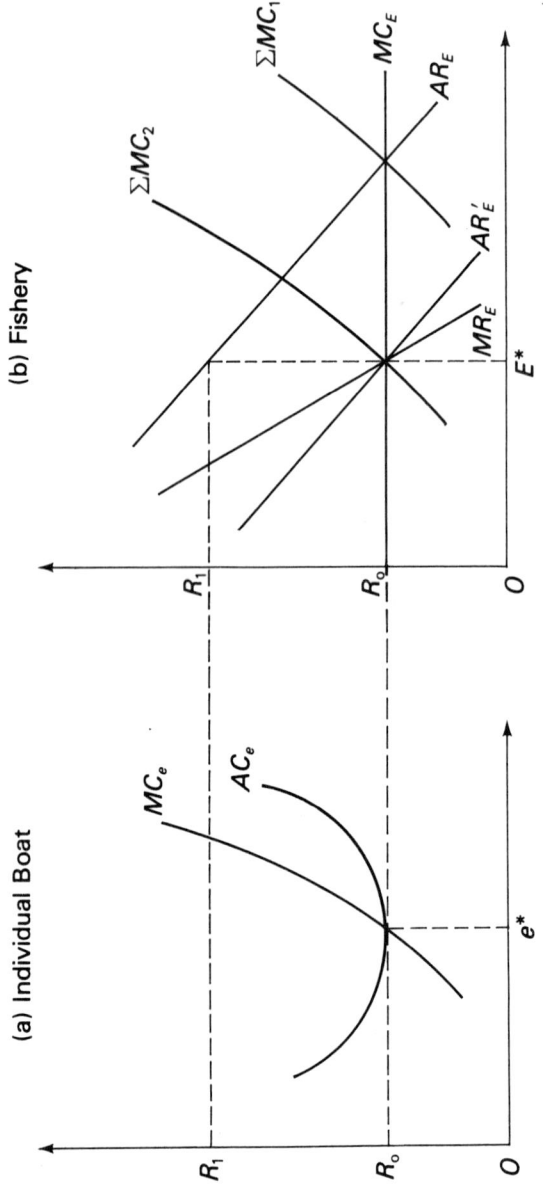

(a) Individual Boat

(b) Fishery

Figure 14.8

Question 21 Will the tax be equally effective if skills are unequal?

Question 22 Using the criteria you set out in answer to Question 10, evaluate these various alternatives and decide which method of regulation you think should be adopted for the herring fishery.

As you will have gathered by now, regulation of a fishery is a very complex problem. In our example it has been simplified by our assumption that only one nation was involved and that fishermen fish for herring and no other species. If fishermen catch more than one species at the same time, there is a problem in the quota form of regulation as fishermen would discard the less valuable species in order to preserve space in their hold for the valuable quota fish. These and other problems need careful consideration, but we do not have time to go into them here. If you are interested in reading further, you could start with the article by Clark (1982) on regulation. The book by Anderson (1977) provides a comprehensive analysis of many aspects of fishing economics and extends the static analysis we have conducted here into a dynamic context. Another useful book on fisheries economics is that by Hannesson (1978). The problem of unequal skills is taken up by Johnson and Libecap (1982) in their article on shrimp fishing in the United States. They also provide an interesting discussion of attempts at regulation by a fishermen's union, and draw attention to the problem of getting fishermen to accept any form of regulation. You may be interested to learn how the European Community proposes to regulate fisheries and, as was mentioned in Part I, Wise (1984) provides a detailed account of the evolution of its policy. If you would prefer a shorter account, try Cunningham and Young (1983).

References

Anderson, Lee G. (1977) *The Economics of Fisheries Management*, Johns Hopkins University Press.
*Clark, Colin W. (1982) 'Models of fishery regulation', in Mirman, Leonard J. and Spulber, Daniel F. (eds.), *Essays in the Economics of Renewable Resources*, North Holland Publishing Company.
Copes, Parzival (1972) 'Factor rents, sole ownership and the optimum level of fisheries exploitation', *Manchester School*, 40, pp. 145—163.
Cunningham, Stephen and Young, James A. (1983) 'The EEC common fisheries policy: retrospect and prospect', *National Westminster Bank Quarterly Review*, May, pp. 2—14.
Hannesson, Rognvaldur (1978) *Economics of Fisheries*, Universitets-forlaget.
*Johnson, Ronald N. and Libecap, Gary D. (1982) 'Contracting problems and regulation: the case of the fishery', *American Economic Review*, 72, pp. 1005—1022.
Wise, Mark (1984) *The Common Fisheries Policy of the European Community*, Methuen.

---

*Suggested supplementary reading.